Safe in
Your
Arms

Safe in Your Arms

A Daughter's Murder—
a Mother's Forgiveness

Nancy Jo Gibson
with Joseph Gibson

Editing and design by Dara Powers Parker

Paperback 979-8-9862456-3-8
E-book 979-8-9862456-4-5

Library of Congress Control Number: 2023915064

PRINTED IN THE UNITED STATES OF AMERICA

ROYAL
RAVEN
BOOKS

In this searing memoir, author Nancy Jo Gibson bares her soul, inviting readers to walk alongside her as she retraces the heart-wrenching events that forever changed her life. With unflinching honesty, Gibson bares the grief that threatened to consume, anger that ignited like a wildfire, and the persistent ache of a mother's shattered dreams. As she confronts the darkness that seemed insurmountable, she finds a true source of solace and healing: the person of Jesus Christ. Guided by a steadfast belief in God's grace, she learns to navigate the treacherous terrain of loss, piecing together her shattered spirit one fragile step at a time.

—Andrew Ray Williams
Pastor, professor, and author of
Reconstructing Prayer (2023)

In Loving Memory of Rebekah Jane Gibson

Many will see what He has done and be amazed.
They will put their trust in the Lord.

PSALM 40:3B

FOREWORD

I had been an advocate for families for the better part of thirty years. From families with special-needs babies to broken children from broken homes. For children who have suffered abuse at the hands of family members or someone outside of their family. For domestic violence and sexual assault victims, I had been an advocate.

My last job, as a Victim Services Coordinator, began in 2002 in our county prosecuting attorney's office. By the end of 2008, after serving close to 400 victims and their families each year, I had begun to question my actual effectiveness in the position of advocate. I was ready to be done and was considering an early retirement the following year.

Then, one night in late January 2009, I was faced with one more challenge that brought me to my knees. I felt lost as to how to advocate for a family in another state, who were about to be thrown into a trauma they had yet to know about.

I am a hands-on, face-to-face person. I like to be able to make eye contact, read body language, and hold the hands of the person hurting. I am a hugger! I prayed—*hard*—for some way to minister to this family who were hours away.

Finally, in the middle of the chaos I was feeling, I heard a Voice that had been silent for far too long. The reason being that I had stopped listening. But I heard these words: *"Faith! Find their faith connection. There is where you start. I will be there. . . ."*

Over the next few years with the Gibson family, I found my reason to continue the work that I had been called to do. I found my way back to my faith. For me, that was where the journey begins.

Thank you, Nancy Jo. You will never know all that you have done for me.

Laura Queen
Former Victim Rights Advocate
for Upshur County, West Virginia

Prologue

Joseph

January 28, 2009

To go to school or to not go to school? That was the major problem confronting me on the morning of January 28, 2009.

It had snowed recently, and I was a college student who commuted about sixty miles to classes. My car was notorious for not doing well in the snow, but I hated missing class. The neighborhood where I lived and had grown up in was located just outside of the city limits. It was always late getting plowed. This time was no exception. I would be on major roads once I got out of the neighborhood, and they were almost certainly already plowed. The temperature was rising too. If I got out of the neighborhood, it would be smooth sailing. Could I get out, though? I looked out my bedroom window at the thick snow, untouched on the street. The decision hung in the air, and my will wavered.

I was a philosophy major and good at overthinking things. If you wanted a spontaneous decision, don't come to me. If you wanted a long-winded argument that arrived at no definite conclusion, I was your man. You know what they say about philosophers: if you lay them all end to end, you still will not reach a conclusion.

The stereotype of philosophers as contemplative, solitary, and cold or unemotional fit fairly well in my case. I must have gotten these traits from my father, as my mother was quite the opposite. She would jump for joy, clap, and squeal in a high-pitched voice whenever something remotely good—and it could be quite remote—happened. If I gave you a thumbs-up, I was probably at near stroke levels of excitement. When my mother would watch *Frosty the Snowman* and Frosty would melt, knowing full well that the cartoon character would be perfectly restored in about three minutes, she would well up with tears and weep. For me, tears were a rather curious and ever-absent phenomena. Why certain unagreeable situations of extreme joy, sorrow, or physical pain should induce a salty wetness to emanate from one's eyes was beyond my comprehension.

But what to do about this snow? My father had made it to work, but he had a truck. My three-year-old niece, Taylor, had been dropped off at our house while her father (my brother) and mother went to work. I started to lean toward trying to make it out. The decision was suddenly made, but it was made in the negative. I opted to stay at home.

That decision would hardly affect my classes or grades at all. However, it had a big impact on my family and on my life. That decision seemed to have been unguided—I had actually wished someone would just tell me what to do—and solely the result of my own will. In reality, it had been guided by loving hands and influenced by a loving and wise will. I was unaware of all of this and decided that the time saved from commuting would best be spent sleeping.

It was still morning, and a phone was ringing in my room. This was in the days of landlines, and everyone had a home phone as well as a cell phone. The ringing was our home phone, and one of the wireless handhelds was in my room. Now, this was most peculiar.

Even someone calling my own cell phone to talk to me would have been odd enough; remember the comment about philosophers being solitary? The call was not for me. The calls were never for me. I generally refused to answer the phone, as it seemed an unnecessary complication. It was much simpler for someone else—someone for whom there was a reasonable chance that the call was for them—to pick it up in the first place.

The call was not for me. But the phone rang again. How did that handheld get in my room anyway? (I never did get the answer to that question.) I decided I would answer the phone, hand it to my mother—the call was probably for her—get the cursed thing out of my room, and then start my day.

Unforeseen hands were again at work.

1.

THE PHONE CALL

Nancy Jo

January 28, 2009

Joseph never, *ever* answered the phone. I could be elbow-deep in dishwater, down on my hands and knees, scrubbing the floor, and he would not answer the phone—even if he were sitting right beside it. His reasoning was equally sound and frustrating: it was never for him. But on this Wednesday morning in January, sequestered in his room with his schoolwork, my twenty-two-year-old son chose to answer the phone.

I remember being shocked and yet ever so grateful that I could continue without interruption. My three-year-old granddaughter, Taylor, and I were at the dining room table, mixing up a dry chai tea recipe. (We do so love our teas!) I was measuring and handing Taylor ingredients, which she dumped into the mixing bowl, while trying to make sure most of it made it *into* the bowl. In the midst of this, the phone rang. I let Taylor finish pouring in the latest ingredient and was about to lift her off the chair so I could get to the phone. Before I could do so, Joseph answered it in his room.

We had awakened to a blanket of snow in our little Shenandoah Valley community of Waynesboro, Virginia. I supposed Joseph had decided to work from home instead of making his usual commute to Liberty University in Lynchburg, where he was a student. He probably could have made it out to the main roads, which would have been cleared by this time, but he chose to sleep in.

He didn't call me to pick up the kitchen extension, and I never thought twice about it. Some time later, Joseph came into the dining room to tell me that our dear friends Henry and Virginia Wingfield would be coming over. My response was worry about the house not being tidy, as I had not been expecting guests.

"It'll be okay, Momma," he said.

Taylor and I continued working on our tea, and Joseph disappeared to our basement.

The timeline is fuzzy to me now, and I'm not sure of the exact order of events. I don't remember how I got there, but I found myself sitting in the living room with Henry and Joseph, making small talk but knowing something was not right. Virginia had gone downstairs with Taylor. When my daughter-in-law, Jennifer, Taylor's mother, came in with tears and kissed me on my cheek, it hit me: *I know exactly what is wrong!*

The night before, we had received a call from the police in Buckhannon, West Virginia. They were looking for our twenty-year-old daughter, Rebekah, and a young man she had been seen with named Ridge. We hadn't even known she was in West Virginia. . . .

Rebekah had been hanging out with Ridge for a little more than a month. Although he lived near us with a foster family, he was the brother of her roommate in West Virginia, where she had been living for the past two years. Rebekah met him when he had come to visit his father and brother at Thanksgiving. He brought her home to us for Christmas, and we had seen him a few times when he came to take her out.

There was something about Ridge that I did not trust. I had pleaded with Rebekah to not go out with him, but she did not listen. I was uncomfortable enough that one day when he came by, I wrote down the make and model of his car as well as the license plate number: a white Nissan (I don't remember the model) with Virginia plates.

The lovely Christmas I had envisioned with Rebekah home never materialized as she was out all hours with

Ridge. I, full of tremendous disappointment and resentment, withdrew. I am ashamed to admit that this withdrawal had been my modus operandi when those I loved did not do what I thought they should—the "right" thing. I never stopped loving them, but I would withdraw that show of love in what I now understand was a passive-aggressive attempt to manipulate them. Oh, how I long to be able to undo my ugly, self-righteous responses . . . especially that Christmas.

We had welcomed Rebekah home, full of hope that she was on a solid "right" track. We envisioned her finding a job, joining us at church, partaking in family dinners, enjoying her little niece—all the things we had longed for and missed for two years. Instead, there was constant conflict and hurt as she had precious little to do with us, choosing rather to be with Ridge and most certainly abusing alcohol. I feared she was using drugs again. Yet I know my withdrawal and—to be blunt—unkindness hurt Rebekah. She moved out of our house and in with a friend in mid-January.

During that time, unbeknown to us, Rebekah was trying to stay away from Ridge. But in late January, she had accepted a ride with him to go back to West Virginia to collect her belongings. On January 27, 2009, she and Ridge were in a Walmart in Buckhannon when Rebekah ran into a guy she knew. She chatted with him and gave him her phone number. (We are not certain, but we think she was trying to get help.)

Ridge was filled with jealous rage. He stalked out to the parking lot and beat the man's car with a baseball bat. Ridge fled the scene with Rebekah before the police arrived. That evening was when we received the call from the Buckhannon police department; they were concerned for Rebekah's safety as well as with criminal charges against Ridge. My husband, David, asked me to look for my note with the license plate number, which he shared with the police.

I went to bed, prayed for Rebekah, and slept soundly all through the night. When I woke, I spent my quiet time with the Lord, as usual. This is the prayer I wrote in my journal that Wednesday morning, January 28:

Father, may Your will be done concerning Rebekah! You alone know what it is going to take to turn her life around. Work in every aspect, Lord, I pray in Jesus's name. I ask that You guard her life and that You save her soul and transform her into a woman of God.

Yes, I knew exactly what was wrong when my husband, David, who had unexpectedly come home from work, still dressed in his UPS browns, sat beside me on the couch. I knew exactly what he would say. My prayers had been answered. The police had found Rebekah, and she was in jail.

But that was okay. It would not be fun or easy, but now, we would be able to get her into a Christian rehabilitation program and counseling. Now, we would be able to help her turn her life around, to heal from all the hurts to her heart and soul.

Everyone seemed to be expecting me to fall apart, but I was okay. I knew that this, although certainly not my desire for my beloved daughter, was the Lord's answer to all my prayers. I actually felt hopeful!

And so I was completely, utterly unprepared when David wrapped his arms around me and said, "He killed her! Ridge killed Rebekah!"

. . .

Deep guttural screams rose from the depths of my soul. I screamed, "NO, NO, NO!" Sobs overwhelmed me. I could not breathe. My ribcage was sore for days afterward from the anguish that ripped through and shattered my heart into a billion pieces.

I was not okay, and I knew I would never, ever be okay again.

My beautiful girl! My baby girl! My Rebekah. . . .

She was gone. She was dead. She was—

Murdered.

Brutally slain.

By Ridge Huffman.

2.

"I Can't Believe It's a Girl!"

1988–2003

When I found out I was pregnant again, I was ecstatic. This would be our third baby in three and a half years. People thought we were crazy, but I loved being pregnant and having babies and toddlers. I had wanted all my life to be a wife and a mommy. Now I was both.

We had two precious little boys: David III, whom we called Davy, and Joseph Emerson. But we longed for a little girl. The whole family was hoping for a girl, but in my heart, I *knew* I was carrying another little boy. I felt like I was letting everyone down. David's sister Susan gave us a tiny, frilly Christmas stocking for the baby, and I felt guilty accepting it. I tried explaining to David that God had a special reason for giving us three little boys.

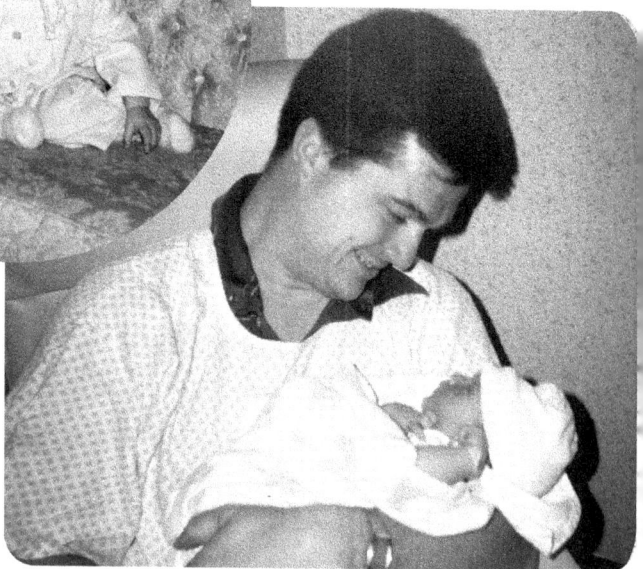

The day of the birth, April 23, 1988, after five hours of labor, I was in shock when the doctor announced, "It's a girl!" I spent the entire three days in the hospital saying over and over, "I can't believe it's a girl!" We were all thrilled to pieces and lavished with all things frilly and pink.

Davy had been a bit of a fussy baby, but not terrible. Joseph had been the most laidback, easy-going baby *ever*. Rebekah . . . well, it seemed Rebekah cried *all* the time. And these were clearly cries of pain. I rarely got more than two to three hours of sleep before she awakened screaming. Nursing satisfied her some, but never for very long. I was so exhausted that when I sat down to nurse her, I would fall asleep, even in the presence of company! Rebekah was a little thing, but she seemed to be growing just fine. The doctor said it was colic and that she would grow out of it.

Months passed, and the screaming did not abate. I would walk the floor with her for an hour and a half, yet nothing I did eased her pain. I would eventually wake David up, fearful that something was seriously wrong. But within minutes of taking her in his arms, he would be cradling a peaceful, sleeping baby. That was until the next screaming spell hit.

When Rebekah wasn't crying, she was such a happy baby girl. She loved her brothers, her daddy, and her mommy! She would laugh at her brothers' silly antics, and she continued to grow and develop, although she did not crawl until almost a year old. David's mom noticed that when Rebekah sat on the floor with her toys, she would pick at her tummy. We knew her stomach was not right, but nothing came of repeated trips to the doctor, who finally referred us to a pediatric practice. But they had no real answers either.

(One of the doctors was very unkind to me, saying that nothing was wrong with Rebekah and that I should just accept that I had a fussy baby. Since then, I have advised mothers to never disregard their instinct if it told them something was wrong with their child, even if the doctors cannot come up with a diagnosis.)

Rebekah also endured chronic ear infections until she had tubes put in, after which she only had one. This was a huge relief—at least the pain of earaches was gone. But the bouts of screaming did not end, though they did come less frequently.

One day, when Rebekah was in the midst of painful screaming, she suffered what we thought was a seizure. She fell completely limp, her tiny tongue lolled out of her mouth, and I could not wake her for a minute or two. I called the doctor's office, and upon my description of the episode, they told me to come in immediately. David's mom came to take care of the boys, and Davy, who had listened to my frantic call to the doctor, informed his grandmother that Rebekah's tongue had fallen out of her mouth. I can only imagine what that image looked like in his young mind!

Having suspected a seizure, the doctor made a referral to a University of Virginia pediatric gastroenterologist. I took Rebekah, praying desperately for answers and that nothing was terribly wrong with our little girl. After ruling out anything serious with a variety of tests over the next couple of weeks, the diagnosis came: irritable bowel syndrome (IBS) since birth.

So many emotions flooded me. Tears of gratitude and relief flowed. It was nothing dangerous, but something she would most likely outgrow. The treatment was as simple as adding Citrucel to Gatorade, a concoction that she called "Yay-Yay." We now understood that the screaming episodes occurred when her bowels spasmed, causing excruciating pain. The spasms rarely lasted longer than ninety minutes, which was often about the time I became desperate and handed her over to David and why she would quiet so quickly thereafter. She hadn't had a seizure at all but had passed out from the pain. Great gratitude welled up in me, although I must admit to the frustration I felt because it had taken so long to obtain an accurate diagnosis.

Despite that, the Citrucel made a difference immediately, and Rebekah began to thrive.

Honestly—although I am perhaps a tad biased—Rebekah was a delightful little girl. She had a most remarkable way of expressing herself.

With three little ones on a single income, we did a lot of consignment shopping. (And truth be told, I can't imagine paying for new children's clothes that are so quickly outgrown or ruined.) One day, Rebekah received a new—as in *brand*-new—outfit. When someone complimented it, she thanked them and let them know that no one had ever worn it before her! Another time, she was wearing a cute jumper. When someone said they liked her pretty dress, she again thanked them but explained that it wasn't a dress at all. "It's a hopper," she said, very matter of fact.

Rebekah had a pronounced lisp when she was young. Of course, the family all thought it was adorable. But at an AWANA club meeting one night at church, some boys made fun of her. She retorted, "How would you wike it if you couldn't talk wight and someone made fun of you?"

A "girly" girl, Rebekah played dress-up and loved dolls—American Girl dolls (her favorite) as well as Barbies. She was passionate about horses and became a very good rider in her early teens, attending a 4-H horse camp for homeschoolers and taking riding lessons. Although petrified at first, she grew to love the water. I have pictures of Rebekah's swimming lessons in which the other children line the side of the pool, holding on while kicking in the water. Rebekah, however, is lying on the cement with just her toes in the water.

I homeschooled my children, and Rebekah was an excellent student, excelling in every subject, except for math. On most of her notebooks, she wrote, "I HATE MATH." She was quite the perfectionist. When she was in kindergarten or first grade, if I put a happy sticker or smiley face on her paper and she hadn't made 100 percent, she would tear it off.

Perfectionism exhibited in her piano-playing as well. If she made a mistake when practicing a piece, even if she was at the very end, she would start completely over from the beginning. It drove me crazy! Rebekah was musically gifted and could play quite well by ear. We loved playing duets together.

From the time she was a tiny child, Rebekah was an animal lover: cats, dogs, horses, mice, and even squirrels! She was first introduced to her grandparents' pet dog, Snookums, whom all the children called "Nook-Nook." Rebekah loved Nook-Nook, but the grumpy little dachshund was not overly fond of her. We later had three dogs while Rebekah was growing up. The first was Binkley, a Jack Russell terrier. Rebekah, though only six, loved teaching this rambunctious little pup new tricks, cuddling him, and playing with him. When Binkley died (much too early, when injured by a neighbor's dog), it was Rebekah who went with me to the SPCA and picked out the most adorable black puppy.

Ronald Anne—part black lab and part basset hound—turned out to be the sweetest dog. She looked exactly like a Labrador when lying down, but the moment she stood up, her short legs and big feet gave away the basset in her. Rebekah tried to teach Ronald Anne tricks, but as sweet as she was, and *very* obedient, she was not so smart. Still, she was greatly loved by Rebekah and everyone who met her.

We allowed Rebekah to adopt her own dog, Opus, when she was about thirteen. Opus was another SPCA rescue puppy, who turned into a big, fluffy, mischievous pet. He was exclusively Rebekah's dog; he slept in her bed and adored her. He also adored stealing her underwear. She would get so irritated to find her bras and underwear in the living room. One evening, she was mortified when the church youth group came over and Opus had left her bra in the middle of the floor for all to see!

Opus had what our vet thought might be Cushing's disease, and we had to have him put to sleep when he was only four years old. Rebekah was devastated and felt like she had "killed her dog."

Rebekah loved cats too. When she was about nine years old, a feral kitten was trapped in our garage. Rebekah tried to coax it to come to her, but it hissed and tried to escape. She fetched a pair of her daddy's gloves, scooped it up, and brought it into the house. This was a Friday afternoon, so we put it in a box and gave it a little food, just until we could take it to the SPCA on Monday. But Ragamuffin, aka "Muffy," never made it to the SPCA. In our home to stay, he grew more and more loving, maturing into the most magnificent, big, buff-colored cat.

While Rebekah never met an animal she didn't love, I have always been terrified of mice. When Rebekah wanted a pet mouse, I was very much against it, but I finally relented with pressure from her and her daddy. We visited a pet store, where Rebekah picked out a mouse that was being sold as snake food. She named it Ralph, and he was a devoted pet. As I write this, I expect it will not be believed, and I admit that if I had not seen it with my own eyes, I would be skeptical too. But Rebekah would take Ralph out in the yard and sit down. When she let him scamper around on the grass beside her, that little mouse would always climb back up onto her lap!

One night, we returned from church to find poor little Ralph stretched out on the kitchen floor. We believe that Muffy had gotten him out of his cage and scared him to death, as there was not a mark on him. Rebekah's heart was broken.

Then there was the time that Davy, Rebekah's oldest brother, found three tiny feral kittens in our woodpile. He waited until David came home and asked if he could show them to Rebekah and me. By that time, there were only two, and we guessed they were barely a day old, with eyes shut and ears down.

We did not expect them to survive but felt it would be better for them to be warm and cared for than starved or poisoned. So, Rebekah, being the night owl that she was as a teenager, took the night shift, and I took the day shift. They were so small that we had to feed them with an eyedropper until they could drink from bottles. With our tender, diligent care, the kittens lived.

We named the black and dark-gray kitten Hodgepodge and the smaller, light-gray and white kitten Gandalf the Gray. However, when we took them to the vet for checkups, we learned that Gandalf was actually a girl! Our granddaughter Taylor, who was two years old at the time, renamed her Kitty. Rebekah claimed Hodgepodge as hers, and he grew into a beautiful cat who was bossy, possessive, and willing to eat anything.

Davy, Joseph, and Rebekah were typical siblings: they loved each other, played together, stood up for each other . . . and fought each other! The boys favorite torment was to take their sister's beloved stuffed animals, hang them from the ceiling fan or in other precarious positions, and build traps so that they fell on her head when she opened her door. They called themselves the "Stuffed Animal Mafia." This infuriated Rebekah, and when the roughhousing caused one of her favorite animals to begin losing its tail, her daddy finally put a stop to it.

We had a lovely maple tree in our front yard—just perfect for little boys to climb but too far off the ground for young Rebekah to reach the lowest branch. One day, her two brothers and a friend invited Rebekah to join them in the tree. She was ecstatic when they helped her climb up the branches. Her smile soon turned to tears, as once they had her positioned, the three boys ran off to play elsewhere. Working in the house, I was unaware of her predicament, and she remained in the tree a while before her daddy came home and rescued her, at which point the boys' smiles turned to tears!

Our nephew Henry was born when Rebekah was two years old. We were blessed to care for him when he was a baby and toddler, and the bond between Henry and Rebekah was exceptional. He was more of a brother than a cousin to all three of our children. Henry and Rebekah played together, but they also loved to sit in the same chair and watch shows. We have many photographs of the two of them sitting together in a chair at all ages.

Just like siblings, they could get into plenty of mischief. On the ceiling above one of the chairs they liked to sit in, some spray-can cheese mysteriously appeared one day. One of Henry's favorite memories was when Rebekah took him on a treasure hunt around our yard, where they came across all kinds of goodies buried underground in different places. It was years before he realized that Rebekah had hidden them all for him to find.

Rebekah was very much a "mommy's girl." When she was little, we played dolls and games and read book after book after book. She never outgrew her love of reading. As she got older, we watched movies together and had our favorites that we watched again and again. We enjoyed scrapbooking, sometimes shopping (although neither of us were big shoppers), cooking side by side, and playing piano.

When she entered her mid-teen years, however, we didn't see eye to eye so well.

3.

THE DAM BURSTS

Joseph

January 28, 2009

"Hello?"

"Is this David Gibson?"

Like I said, the phone call wasn't for me. "No."

"May I please speak to David or Nancy Jo?"

"May I please ask who is calling?"

"This is Ridge's brother."

"May I ask what this is about?"

"He killed her. Ridge killed Rebekah."

. . .

I don't know how long it took me to answer, but I was suddenly given a lot of information to digest. My first thoughts turned to my mom and my niece in the dining room. I quickly decided that handing the phone to my mom while my niece watched and listened was not the thing to do. Maybe the call *was* meant for me, though no one could have known this at the time. It needed to be kept quiet—for now.

My next thought was—please don't judge me too harshly—*Shouldn't the police be calling about something like this?* I grew somewhat skeptical, but I knew that if this were true, it would be much worse than Frosty melting. I then decided that one of the first things to do was confirm this information.

"Thank you for letting me know. Do you have a number for the police department there?"

"Ummm . . . I can get it for you. I'm so sorry."

"Thank you for saying so, and I appreciate the help."

I got the number, received some more apologies—which I accepted as graciously and reassuringly as I could—and hung up.

Then, I quickly constructed a more detailed plan. (1) Instantly erect a dam to hold back all emotions and personal feelings. There would be time for that later. Right now, they would only muddle things. (This step was mostly subconscious and had begun immediately upon hearing the news). (2) Call some people to pray. (3) Confirm the information. (4a) Tell family members and the people praying. (4b) Arrange for someone to come and watch my niece. (5) Tell my mom.

My little niece, Taylor, came into the room and asked to play. I told her I was busy, and she really needed to leave me alone right now. She smiled and walked out of the room.

I called some close family friends, who were good, godly people, and I confirmed the news with the police. I won't go into all the details of calling family and friends; it was hard, but the dam held up. Perhaps the hardest was telling my father. He began driving home from work, and our friends from church, Henry and Virginia Wingfield, began to drive to the house to watch my niece. My main concern at this point was what to do if the arrivals of the two parties were too divergent.

Unseen hands were still at work; my father and Henry and Virginia arrived at the same time. Virginia led my niece downstairs, and the rest of us went in the living room.

My father told my mother.

Frosty melted, and my dam burst.

4.

"What Do We Do Now?"

Nancy Jo

January 28–30, 2009

On the other end of that phone call, which Joseph had inexplicably answered that late January morning, was Ridge's brother with the news that Ridge had murdered Rebekah. Like I said before, Joseph never answered the phone, and yet this day, he did. This intervention could have only been the grace and mercy of God.

Joseph, most certainly led and empowered by the Holy Spirit, hung up and dialed the Buckhannon Police Department to verify what he had been told. Once the police confirmed that Ridge had murdered his sister, Joseph began making other phone calls: to his dad, who was mercifully close to the UPS headquarters; to his brother, Davy, and his wife, Jennifer; to our friends Henry and Virginia Wing-field; to David's and my sisters; among others.

I am still in awe of this young man and the precise, mature, and wise decisions he made that day. His incredible inner strength and love for me enabled him to shield me until I was surrounded by those who loved me.

After David, Jennifer, and the Wingfields arrived at the house, more support was to come. Davy, our twenty-four-year-old son and Taylor's daddy, came moments later. David's sisters, Susan and Beth; Renee, who I consider my sister, although she is much more than even that; and one of our pastors, Shane Lilly, joined us. We were all in shock, and I truly don't remember a lot, but there are several scenes I do recall with crystal clarity:

- My cousin Sandra, who is in a wheelchair from polio, lets me sit on her lap, like my daddy, who was also wheelchair-bound, would have done.
- Pastor Shane jumps in to take care of funeral-home and other details.
- Ridge's foster dad and foster brother, who live nearby, come and tell us what they know: that Ridge had sliced Rebekah's throat. I cry and pray for Ridge with them.
- Once things settle a bit, I realize I am going to have to tell my mother. With dread, I call and ask her to come to the house—that we have some news about Rebekah. Her knees buckle when we tell her.

- Food is brought, and I manage to get a couple of bites down a dry, constricted throat without choking.
- Renee, Beth, and Susan gather up piles of used tissues and take them to the kitchen trash.
- I am given a Xanax.
- More family and friends arrive throughout the day. I sit like a weeping stone on the couch. I don't know if I talk, and if I do, if it makes any sense.

I don't remember going to bed that night, but I do remember waking up the next morning and getting dressed. Seeing our dear sisters still at our side, I remember asking them, "What do we do now? Just sit and wait for people to arrive?"

My journal entry from January 29:

O Lord Jesus, we need You! O Lord Jesus—I cannot bear this grief. Father God, I am desperately clinging to the hope that Rebekah is with You and Satan has been defeated in her life once and for all—that she is at peace, full of joy and everlasting life, aware at last of how much YOU LOVE HER. I cling to the thought of Daddy and [David's] Mom being there to greet her, Lord God. O Jesus, my baby girl. O Jesus, help me and

David and Mama, Davy and Joseph, to cling to You—do not leave our side for an instant, O Lord God Almighty. Somehow bring good out of this—good for us—glory for Your Name—defeat for Satan.

Over the next few days, we gradually learned more details. But before I share them here, I must make a disclaimer: I do not know all the specifics, and I have purposefully not sought them out. I still do not read any media reports about it, and my husband and others are careful to shield me from them. And so the following details are *my* understanding only, but this is the gist of what happened.

After beating the other man's car with a bat and fleeing the scene, Ridge had driven Rebekah back to the Buckhannon Walmart parking lot. He had gotten her as drunk as possible, and he was intoxicated as well. He took an empty liquor bottle and hit her over the head. He then cut her throat.

I don't know if all this occurred outside or inside his vehicle. I do know that she ended up in the passenger seat of his vehicle, the white Nissan, with a blanket thrown over her. He drove to a gas station/convenience store and bought cigarettes, then he drove to his father's house in Buckhannon. The morning of January 28, Ridge's father came into their living room, found Ridge asleep on the couch, and asked him what had happened. He said, "I think I killed someone last night."

I will be eternally grateful that Ridge's father immediately called the police. He could have tried to hide Rebekah's body or helped Ridge go on the lam, but he chose to call the police. Sergeant Doug Loudin, who had been looking for Ridge and Rebekah all night, responded to the call.

What he saw when he removed the blanket from Rebekah's body was traumatizing. It impacted him for life, he said. Again, I thank God that Sergeant Loudin was the one to find her. He stayed with her body until they were ready to release her to the medical examiner, and he rode beside her on the way to the medical facility. Even fourteen years later, I cannot write this without tears of gratitude flowing. That Sergeant Loudin respected and protected Rebekah's body in this way still means so much to us. My heart cannot even comprehend the anguish of those victims' families whose stories are tragically different.

During those first days, I surely only survived by the grace of God, who enlisted the right people to minister to us. We are ever grateful for the precious friends and family who surrounded us in love, support, and practical help.

David and I felt totally overwhelmed and had no idea what to do.

I have been so kindly cushioned from the full, unbearable truths of the damage Ridge inflicted upon our beautiful daughter. I remember very clearly sitting on our couch, David and our sisters gathered close, being told that the injuries to Rebekah's body were so severe that they did not know if we would be able to see her before we buried her. This was yet another horror and completely unexpected. Waves of grief, sorrow, anger, and uncontrolled sobbing rose up again. I asked what exactly Ridge had done to our daughter. I believe Susan gave me another Xanax at this point.

Our relief in hearing from our funeral home director, Charles Reynolds, that we would be able to see Rebekah was *immense.* How we thank the Lord for this kindness and Mr. Reynolds's expertise. I had been to a funeral where our loved one's body had first gone to the medical examiner, and their skin had been discolored. It had been so upsetting to me then, and I was fearful that Rebekah's body would look the same. I shared my fear, and I don't remember how things played out, but Mr. Reynolds had already contacted the medical examiner and explained the procedures to take so that the discoloration would not be noticeable.

Pastor Brandon, our church's lead pastor, visited and shared that he had spoken with Rebekah at the Christmas Eve service. He was completely confident that she was with Jesus. He said that she had known her lifestyle was not right and that she'd wanted out of it, but she just couldn't find the way. How desperately we needed this word, and how thankful we were for his tenderness!

Even in those first hours and days, we had to deal with thoughtless and unkind people, some of whom were *family* members. People questioned us about gory details, and others jumped on the opportunity to spread the news with no thought about how we would be impacted.

No matter where we are in life, there are those who will cause us much pain, even when we are already hurting beyond measure. We can either dwell on those hurts, or we can cling in gratitude to those the Lord sends to lift us up and love us with His love. We must do the latter and consider these experiences as lessons that teach us not to hurt others in their time of sorrow.

We were told by someone that very day that they didn't know if Rebekah was in heaven because she had been caught up in a wrong lifestyle. Another person had the audacity to inform my mother that Rebekah was in hell. And these were *church* people! Oh, the truth in the saying that Christians are the only ones who shoot their own wounded!

We can be experts at ranking sins. I was certainly one of the worst: clearly seeing, criticizing, and condemning

Rebekah's external sins and struggles and judging her for them while being utterly blinded to my own internal sins, as well as the wounded souls my sins left in my wake. Some Christians see God as having limitless grace and mercy for the lost but expecting His followers to toe the line and never falter or fail. It is with deep sorrow that I confess that I was one of those Christians. But I have come to more fully grasp the truth that I am just as desperate for God's grace and mercy. Furthermore, my sins of pride and self-righteousness were no less abhorrent to God than Rebekah's sins of promiscuity and substance abuse.

My calendar verse on January 30 was Mark 14:38: "The spirit truly is ready, but the flesh is weak" (KJV). That verse, I believe, came straight from the Lord's heart to assure me that Rebekah was indeed in heaven. I heard the Lord saying, *"Rebekah's spirit knew, loved, and longed to follow Me, but her flesh was so weak that she would have always struggled. So, in My grace and mercy, I set her free from her flesh. Be at peace, My child; your daughter is with Me."*

While I reached out and cried out to God for comfort, I also struggled with the feeling that He had not heard my desperate prayers for Rebekah.

5.

REBELLION

2004–2008

To be honest, as a parent, I was overly controlling, too harsh a disciplinarian, and too quick to judge. I was this way with all three of my children, and my heart aches to not be able to do things over with each of them.

I had been a very compliant child, raised in a strict home that was also filled with lots of love. Both my parents were greatly involved in my life, and while strict, their rules were fair. Being one who wanted to please my parents—especially my daddy—I thrived in the thick of rules that most of my classmates did not have to follow. I am to this day very much a rule-follower, and I long to please those I love. David was also raised in a very strict home, where he was very loved, but not in the warm, embracing, playful way that I was.

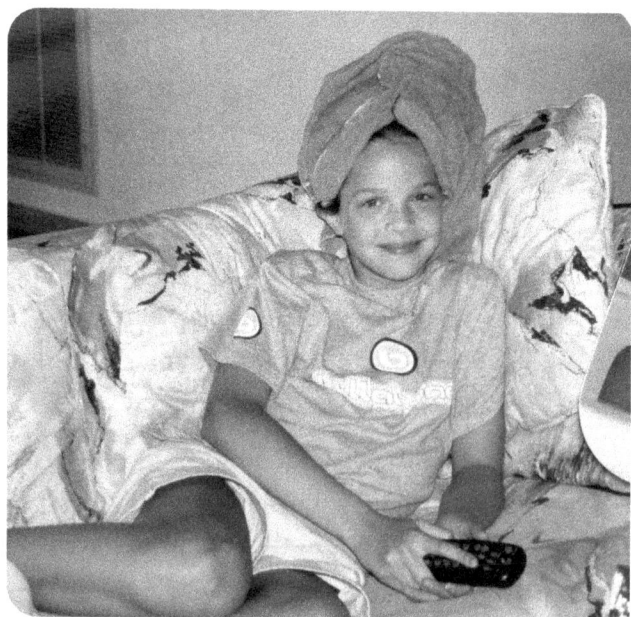

It is so true that we raise our children in large part the way we were raised . . . or we veer far from it. David and I stayed true to the stricter parenting that we knew, and this worked well for our Joseph, who was extremely compliant. It did not work so well for our Davy and Rebekah, however, who were both strong-willed. As a mother, I did not know how to give and take—to give freedoms bit by bit so that my children could learn to navigate the difficulties of life and learn from their mistakes while also under the protection of our home.

I was very rigid in my thinking/parenting, and to be blunt, I expected all three of our children to march to the beat of my drum and to do so unerringly. Little slip-ups were expected, of course, but bigger ones were met with a harshness that greatly grieves me today. As Davy and Rebekah grew older, I seemed only to notice their misbehavior, rebellion, and outward sin.

I was overly critical and extremely judgmental. I was more concerned with their behavior than their hurting hearts and exploring where the behavior was coming from. I was extremely passive-aggressive in my confrontation of disobedience and wrong choices. While I never, ever stopped loving them, I would withdraw the expressions of my love as punishment, expecting them to respond as I would have to *my* mother when I messed up. But they were not the people-pleasers that I was.

What did this withdrawal look like? For one, I refused to be overly affectionate. I would become quiet and avoid interacting with my children. Once their choices became out-and-out wrong—rather than simple disobedience—I became less and less loving mother and more and more harsh judge. Only because they were older, I had no more power or control to back up my judgments.

I may go so far as to say that I was an immature and powerless judge. I sat upon my "bench" and judged not just behaviors and wrongdoings but also my precious children themselves. I was critical, unkind, unmerciful, self-righteous, and completely oblivious to the pain my children were in—some of that pain being from wounds I had caused. David was perhaps not as harsh in some ways, but more so in others; he was also at work almost all of our waking hours.

Looking back, I see no excuses, no license for my behavior. But I also see a mother who was exhausted, who felt very much alone, and who had no idea how to truly love a rebellious child. Many of the Focus on the Family–type parenting tips I encountered and the people I listened and looked up to confused me. Their advice was "If you do your job right, your children will stay close to God and walk in His ways."

Now, there is great tension here! I would tell you that I *did* teach my children what was right. They knew God's Word and not only His laws but His love. I was actively involved in their lives from the moment they entered this world. As a homeschool mom, I was also their teacher. We played together, ate together, learned together, worked

together, served others together, took trips together. . . . I
was the best mommy I knew how to be, and in many ways,
I believe I mothered well. But they were each their own
person. Even parents who are much better than I was still
have children who rebel. (Recently, I heard someone say
that if we are tempted to judge someone by how their children turned out, consider God, who is the perfect parent,
and how His children have turned out!)

Parents have a great responsibility to love their children and teach them—not just life skills but also right
from wrong. Even so, our children still have free will, and
they choose for themselves as they mature which paths to
follow. When children of any age make poor choices, they
need to know that their parents still love them. In fact,
they need to know it at these times even more!

This is where my greatest failures lie. When Rebekah
started having sex, smoking cigarettes, and using pot,
I had a difficult time seeing past these behaviors to my
beloved daughter, who still needed her mother's love and
tender care. She needed to know that I was *for* her, not
against her, even though she was making choices I was
not for.

When she moved in with her boyfriend at the time, I
refused to visit their apartment, even when she asked me
to, for fear that I would be seen as condoning the situation.
This is one example of a multitude of choices that I so
wish I could go back and do differently. The fact of the
matter is that Rebekah's heart was still soft. Her wrong-

doing was easy to see; yet, she still loved God, while I was like a white-washed tomb! I also loved God, but I was following rules on the outside while being ugly and hard-hearted on the inside.

Jesus tells a story in the Gospels about a religious teacher who went to church one day to pray. He told God about how good he was and all the things he did for Him. He thanked God that he was not like other people who do wrong, such as cheaters and adulterers. And then, looking to see who else was in church, he spotted a tax collector. Tax collectors worked for the government of Rome, and they were despised by the Jewish people as traitors. To make matters worse, tax collectors were often very wealthy, charging more taxes than were owed and keeping the extra for themselves. When the teacher saw the tax collector, he thanked God that he was not like him.

The religious teacher had barged right up to the front of the church and boldly addressed God, distancing himself from the other, "unrighteous" people. The tax collector, on the other hand, stood in the back, too aware of his wrongdoings to even look up to heaven. Instead of looking around at the others, the tax collector looked inside himself and, beating his chest, cried out, "God, have mercy on me, a sinner!"

Jesus went on to say that it was the tax collector who left forgiven that day, not the teacher, who was just as guilty and just as needy of God's mercy, grace, and forgiveness, but with internal, hidden sin rather than obvious, external sin.

Why do I tell this story? Because it is an apt picture of Rebekah and me. I was such a "good little girl" and later, a "good" woman. I have never smoked, done drugs, been promiscuous, stolen anything, or even gotten a speeding ticket (although not because I never deserved one). I failed to understand that my sins and critical spirit were equally offensive to God as Rebekah's more obvious rebellion: the story of the religious teacher and the tax collector brought to life in 2008.

The film *The Passion of the Christ* came out when Rebekah was beginning her teenage rebellion. David and I went to see this incredible and deeply moving portrayal of Jesus's sacrifice. Instead of focusing on my own sin, I thought of all the people I wished would see it and take to heart its depiction of the agony Jesus suffered for their sins.

When Rebekah saw it, I asked her what she thought about it. She said, "Momma, I will never see that movie again."

Defensively, I asked, "Why in the world not? It was a good movie!"

She replied, "I cannot bear to see what *my* sin did to Jesus."

6.

THE FUNERAL

January 31–February 4, 2009

I had helped plan my father's funeral five years before and
that was hard enough. But to plan your *child's* funeral?
Absolutely excruciating.

Reynolds Hamrick Funeral Home—Charles Reynolds
in particular—was such a blessing to us. They were so
kind and patient. But the truth was that we were financially unprepared for a funeral. When we went to look at
caskets, our momma and daddy hearts ached to provide
the very best for our girl. We examined all the choices and
prices. David, his father-provider role crumbling, asked
with embarrassment if there were any less expensive
options. We were not made to feel guilty or ashamed. Mr.
Reynolds simply said, "Yes," and we proceeded from there.

In keeping with our limited budget, we asked that a single red rose (Rebekah's favorite flower) be placed on top of the casket. Mr. Reynolds kindly paid for that.

We were not prepared to purchase a cemetery plot either. We chose one that was close to my daddy's burial site, which was a comfort to us. Then we went home. David sold his guns, I sold my jewelry, and with the unbelievably generous monetary gifts from others, we were able to pay for the plot, vault, and other burial expenses.

David's younger sister, Beth, was our loyal support system at every step, taking care of details and making appointments. In fact, Beth and their older sister, Susan, picked out and purchased an outfit for Rebekah, as well as one for myself—even a pair of shoes. To have been spared the anguish of shopping for my dead child's grave clothes was a gift indeed, and they did a wonderful job, choosing an outfit that "was" Rebekah: classy and black. Surely Susan's and Beth's hearts were breaking as they shopped, but what a loving sacrifice.

Then came the day we were allowed to see Rebekah's body in the funeral home. Once again, my dear husband and sisters were so very quick to safeguard me. David, Susan, and Beth went into the room to see Rebekah, while Renee stayed outside with me.

David came out, his face streaming tears but smiling. "It's good," he said. "She is good."

Again, gratitude that we could see Rebekah's body mingled with the agony that it was empty. We would look upon our daughter's face this day and the day of the funeral, and then no more. Never again would we see her, hear her laugh, hug her…. Never again on this earth. I touched her . . . so cold, so lifeless. But she was beautiful, and her lovely face wore an expression of peace.

Susan and Beth gently wrapped Rebekah's hands around a little purse that contained ashes of Mom, David's mother—another tiny comfort for shattered hearts.

Tuesday, February 3: "Family Night" at the funeral home brought a tremendous turnout—more than 450 guests. So many thoughtful things were said. So many loving hugs were given. So many tears were shed. We are so grateful for every kind and loving soul who showed up, some of whom waited hours to see us. We were also so very exhausted by the end of the evening.

One of Rebekah's old boyfriends showed up, and not knowing whether to anticipate trouble, Pastor Shane kept a careful eye on him. Although he had led her down a wrong path and been abusive when drinking, he would not have murdered Rebekah. I believe this is an important distinction because as much as I had despised his influence on my daughter, he showed up because he had cared for her, and I hadn't given him much of a chance. (I pray he has overcome his addictions.)

We felt very strongly that we did not want Rebekah "on show" as a murder victim. We did not want to satisfy people's morbid curiosity, and so we ordered a closed casket for the visitation and the funeral. But even on Family Night, we were hassled by those intent on taking charge and having their way. Some people skipped the line, and others tried to push their way in when, at the end of the evening, the casket was opened for close family only. It is hard not to be resentful at times like that . . . or when writing about it many years later.

Wednesday, February 4: The day of the funeral was clear and frigid. Church on the Hill, in Fishersville, Virginia, was packed, with some attendees having to stand. Again, much of this day is a blur, but I do remember asking Keith Hulton, who had been our faithful pastor for many years, to participate. Having watched Rebekah grow up and being such a positive influence in all our children's lives, Keith was kind enough to share about Rebekah as a little girl. He told about when he would call the house and she would answer the phone, "Hello, dis is Rebekah Jane Gibson peaking."

We also wanted Pastor Brandon Williams of Church on the Hill to share the gospel, which he did, as he always does, with such sincere love and concern for those hearing it. I do clearly remember Pastor Brandon saying, "Some people do not believe there is a devil. After this, how can you not?" And then he pointed to our good, good Father God and the salvation He offers through Christ Jesus. Five people raised their hands to accept Jesus as Savior that day!

Our brother-in-law Jeff Walter had been Rebekah's favorite singer, and so we asked him to sing "Amazing Grace (My Chains Are Gone)" by Chris Tomlin.[1] This song, which blends the old hymn with newer lyrics, so beautifully expresses God's limitless grace. To us, it also conveyed Rebekah's newfound freedom—her chains indeed severed for all eternity!

We also played Meredith Andrews's song "You're Not Alone."[2] I had printed, mounted, and framed the lyrics of this song for Rebekah, which I sent to her along with the CD. She told me she listened to that song over and over. Although I was not able to be with Rebekah at all times, although she felt abandoned by her family, although she struggled through bad choices and poor conduct, and

---

1 Chris Tomlin, "Amazing Grace (My Chains Are Gone)," track 11 on *See the Morning*, Sparrow Records, 2006.

2 Meredith Andrews, "You're Not Alone," track 11 on *The Invitation*, Word Entertainment, LLC, 2008.

although her precious heart was broken again and again, she was *not* alone. The Lord never left her side; He was with her all her life, and He loved her all her life!

The pall bearers included Davy and Joseph; our nephew Henry, with whom Rebekah had been inseparable when they were young; Davy's friend, who we considered our "adopted" son, Jamin Sheard; Rebekah's godfather, Dave Simpson; and Ben Lancaster.

Then we invited the attendees to the burial at Augusta Memorial Park.

Had I the opportunity to do this day over, we would have had a private graveside service and then returned to the church for a celebration of life. It was so cold and blustery that day, but I honestly do not remember that or any other detail from the gravesite, other than concern for Jamin, who was not wearing a warm coat. Some people saw three white geese fly overhead, but I missed it. This would be an unusual sight; in fact, neither I nor they had ever seen it before, and I have never seen it since. It seems to me like a miraculous reminder of the Trinity: God the Father, God the Son, God the Holy Spirit—God with us, even in this place of cruel death and agonizing grief. Although I did not witness the sight myself, I still hold the memory close to my heart.

The funeral and burial having concluded, we went home. Broken, bent beneath sorrow we were never meant to bear, and unsure how to navigate life.

The grief journey had barely begun.

7.

How Did We Get Here?

2004–2008

My failures as a mother and David's absenteeism impacted Rebekah, Davy, and to a lesser degree, Joseph. We did not accurately portray for our daughter how God loved her no matter what, how He was always for her, how He never saw her as less than His beautiful child, saved by grace. Beyond this, I believe the enemy used three major life events to bring confusion, lies, and great harm to Rebekah.

Rebekah was extremely close to both her "Mom-Mom" Gibson (David's mom) and her Granddaddy Lyttle (my daddy). She adored her "Pop-Pop" Gibson (David's dad) and her "Mom-Mom" Lyttle, but she felt a deeper connection with Mom and Daddy.

David's mother had been very strict with her children, but as most grandparents do, she lightened up considerably with her grandchildren. She had so much wisdom and insight and was a grounding place for Rebekah, and for me as well. I think most of all, she understood Rebekah's teenage struggles and was a good sounding board. She had raised two teen girls, and while strict, she was much less rigid in her parenting than my mother had been. Rebekah benefited not only from Mom's understanding but also from Mom's talks with me, as she gently encouraged me to loosen my grip on the reins. Any topic was safe for Rebekah to discuss with Mom-Mom Gibson.

Mom spent time with Rebekah, teaching her to garden (flowers), listening, taking her shopping, and helping her with fashion. Rebekah had a classic sense of fashion when she dressed up. She loved hats and had an Audrey-Hepburn look about her. She never wore makeup but possessed a natural beauty. I think much of this came from Mom-Mom.

Unfortunately, David's mother endured years of progressive physical and mental illness due to Parkinson's. Both her body and mind failed as the disease progressed, and this was difficult for the entire family. Mom died on Mother's Day, 2004. We all grieved greatly, and Rebekah lost a beloved grandparent and confidante.

My daddy was truly the best in the world. In 1968, his helicopter was shot down in Vietnam, resulting in paralysis from the waist down, as well as frayed nerve endings in his spine. Despite chronic pain beyond comprehension and being wheelchair-bound, he was extremely active, both at work and at play. Daddy enjoyed life to its fullest, and he loved deeply. He was so much fun, and all the grandchildren adored being with him.

Rebekah's granddaddy provided a safe refuge, unconditional love, abundant fun and laughter, and many teaching experiences. My parents lived in Georgia while the children were growing up, so Rebekah's time with him was limited to their visits here and ours there, but the bond between the two of them was deep. He and my mother eventually moved close to us when Rebekah was a teenager.

While Mom-Mom was in her final year and a half of Parkinson's, we found out that Daddy had terminal cancer. For paraplegic veterans, colonoscopies were avoided until symptoms of a problem cropped up. By the time his symptoms demanded a colonoscopy, cancer had spread outside the colon wall. Despite chemotherapy, and natural remedies as well, Daddy's cancer had metastasized to his liver, lung, and brain within eighteen months. After losing Mom in May, Daddy died on December 3, 2004.

While Rebekah had been a mommy's girl all during childhood, it was these two grandparents who gave her great stability in her early teens. After losing them, one right after the other, I was caught up in my own grief and did not recognize how my precious daughter was floundering. These two losses—so close together, unexplored at length, and without grief counseling—really rocked Rebekah's foundation and may have contributed to her having lost her way.

Although it may be hard to believe after I've admitted how legalistic and unkind I had been, I have always loved God. I was brought up in church, as was David, and church has always been of great value and importance to us. We raised our children in church, where they had tons of fun and learned about God.

In Rebekah's tumultuous years, our church hired a new youth pastor. He was young, he loved God, and he was as judgmental and critical as I was. He had no patience when Rebekah came to youth group less than enthusiastic and without a smile. While understanding and freely giving grace to those who did not know Jesus, this youth pastor had no grace, kindness, or understanding for Christian teens who stumbled while trying to walk out their faith and do what God tells us in His Word.

CAPTAIN J.F. LYTTLE, Jr.
MEMORIAL PARK & PLAYGROUND

Raised in Mullens, WV.

Graduated from Mullens High School, Class of 1958. Served with distinction in Vietnam, US Army as Company Commander c1/5 1st. Cavalry Division. Received 3 Purple Hearts, Bronze Star and Silver Star. Shot down in helicopter, paralyzed from waist down. Retired from Army as Captain.

Worked at Woodrow Wilson Rehabilitation Center in Waynesboro, Va. As Rehabilitation and Recreation Director. Participated in Wheelchair Olympics, and was Coach of the Va. Wheelchair Olympic Team.

Transferred to Franklin D. Roosevelt Institute for Rehabilitation as the Facilities Director. Became an official for the National Wheelchair Olympics.

Carried the Olympic Torch into Warm Springs in 1996.

Died December 3, 2004
A TRUE HERO OF MULLENS
Dedicated by a Grateful Town.

While I struggled with how this man's and his wife's reactions and unkindness hurt Rebekah, I must also say that they were merely an extension of my own beliefs. When Rebekah shared some of this with me, I should have first believed that her perception of the situation was correct, and then I should have acted on it.

I only share this here for two purposes:

First, it is important to go to a church that understands that even after we accept Jesus as Savior, we are *never* any less needful of God's grace, mercy, forgiveness, and love. And no one—lost or saved—deserves God's grace! He gives it because He loves us. I had no true understanding of the grace of God at this time, and this church merely supported my misconceptions.

Second, when our children and teens raise concerns, we must look into them. Do not assume it is merely their desire to not attend church or youth group. Do not assume the leaders are always right and our kids are wrong. Do not assume our teens are not perceptive or discerning enough to know when something is not right. Make sure your child or teen is genuinely loved and supported within your church and by those who minister to them.

This final blow to Rebekah's sweet soul was perhaps the most devastating. I must say that had I been a better mother, had I handled things differently, it would not have had the destructive force that it did.

I am still not sure when the abuse began, but a family friend hurt Rebekah—sexually as well as physically and mentally. Rebekah eventually shared the abuse with a trusted friend of the family. This wise friend told her that she either had to tell us or they would.

The young man was twenty-one, and Rebekah was only sixteen. We could have pressed charges but chose not to. Family relationships complicated matters, and while we felt we made the right decision, I know that the way I handled the situation was extremely damaging to Rebekah. David and I both had no idea the extent to which Rebekah would suffer as a result of this abuse. It was worse than we had realized.

By not pressing charges, I believe we unintentionally sent a message to Rebekah that what happened was not that bad or significant and that she was not worth the fight. While none of this was true, of course, that didn't sway her perception. Oh, how this grieves me, and I cringe even now while recording it. One thing I know for certain is that while the original source of the damage was extremely destructive, my response prevented my precious child from healing from it.

The counselor we took her to told me personally that Rebekah had been in a position where she simply could not refuse what he was doing to her. She'd had such an emotional attachment to this young man—a crush, so to speak—before the abuse began. She was under his spell and unable to say no.

But I did blame her. I rejected this counselor's insight without exploring it or asking them to help me understand. I felt she knew better and should have resisted. I also felt she should have let us know a whole lot sooner than she did. I was harsh, judgmental . . . and I simply did not see her the same as before.

Only the Lord knows how Rebekah might have weathered the fallout if I had been genuinely on her side. What if I had treated her the way God treats us when we are harmed, or even how He treats us when we are totally to blame for the terrible situations we find ourselves in? He loves us and accepts us unconditionally! If only I had listened to the counselor and sought counsel myself. Again, in hindsight, I am all too aware of my lack of effort to discern what was going on in my sweet daughter's heart.

What I know now came from Rebekah, who confided in me later:

- She felt that the young man got off scot-free; he was able to completely distance himself from what had happened and move on with his life, while she was left to be blamed and broken.
- She saw herself as "less than" from this point on—not worthy of a good, godly man, who would respect and truly love her. She continued to believe this until the

day she died, even though I tried to convince her otherwise.

- The pain in her young heart and soul was so great that she even resorted to self-harm (cutting) for a season.

And although Rebekah did not talk about it, the truth is that every relationship she had after this one was also abusive. There was one man who, I believe, really loved Rebekah (the one who came to her Family Night at the funeral home); but drinking altered his demeanor, and he was abusive then as well. I believe her own alcohol and short-lived drug abuse were attempts to deaden the pain that began with that initial abuse and compounded with my failures and every poor choice she made from then on.

And so an absentee daddy, a legalistic mommy, the loss of two beloved grandparents, and the physical/mental/ sexual abuse that she never recovered from are how I believe we ended up here—our beloved daughter murdered at the hands of another abusive man.

8.

"O God, I'm Floundering!"

February 2009

In the days and months after the loss of Rebekah, our living room became a sanctuary for me. There, I could either pace the floor or sit on the couch, reading my Bible and other books, journaling, praying, crying . . . sobbing. I told God over and over that I was just so sad and that I wanted to go home. To heaven, I meant. My tears had no end. As though my anguish were something I couldn't swallow, my throat would ache and close up, smothering me if I did not release it through sobs. How many boxes of tissues must I have gone through?

One day, I was overwhelmed with grief that turned into rage. Emboldened by my confusion and hurt that God had not rescued my child and saved her life, I began to accuse. God had not done things *my* way. In fact, He seemed to have turned His back on me and a deaf ear to all my prayers for so many years—from the time she was born and even before!

I paced my living room, back and forth, crying and screaming, "God, did You even hear my prayers for Rebekah? Because it sure doesn't seem like You did!"

I had faithfully prayed a protective covering over Rebekah, in Jesus's name. I had prayed for her safety and for her life. I had asked God to work mightily on her behalf. I had cried out for her freedom and joy and purpose and fully restored relationships. And now I had a dead child! Where was God in that? I could not see Him in the pitch-black darkness of grief that I could barely function in and was certain that I would die from.

I did not hear the Holy Spirit's voice, but I did receive the impression that I needed to go back through my prayer journal and highlight all my prayers for Rebekah. As I did this, going back months before her death, I found that my prayers for her could be divided into four broad categories. The words were different, the specifics changed, but the overall cry of my heart to the Lord on behalf of my child remained the same throughout the past months in these four ways. As I examined and organized my journal entries into these categories, my loving heavenly Father showed me that He did indeed hear *and* answer my prayers . . . just not at all the way I had envisioned or expected.

The first was that God would set Rebekah free from Satan's grasp. And God did set her free! Rebekah would *never* be held in the grip of sin again. She was perfect, righteous, and holy. Truly, her chains were forever gone!

Second, that God would draw Rebekah to Himself: I could not very well doubt this one. Rebekah was in the very presence of God; she was face to face with her Savior! She would never feel separated from Him again but would, for all eternity, rest in the fullness of His presence. What a perfect answer to prayer.

Third, that God would safeguard Rebekah's life: Reading this one cut my heart afresh. I had prayed time and time again that God would keep my baby girl safe and that her life would be spared so that she might have abundant life and serve Him. And, of course, I meant that we—her parents—might enjoy her until *we* left Earth for heaven.

This prayer especially caused me to pause and listen to hear what God would say. In His gentle, compassionate, but firm way, the Holy Spirit reminded me that God *had* spared Rebekah's life. He had accomplished this for all eternity when Rebekah accepted Jesus as her Savior and Lord as a little six-year-old girl. Although she had wandered away from God's best path for her, she never stopped believing in Him. She never stopped telling me her plans to help others when she got herself straightened out. She never stopped loving Jesus and feeling the weight of her sin. Neither had she turned her back on her beliefs or rejected what Christ had done for her on the cross.

Rebekah was *not* dead; she had eternal life. In fact, she was more alive than she had ever been! God spared her from death through what His Son had accomplished by dying for her. And He didn't stay dead; He resurrected and defeated death so that Rebekah could live forever with Him.

The last prayer was that Rebekah would be used in a mighty way by God. I prayed that once she returned fully to Him and gained victory over the enemy's designs for her life that she would live according to His purpose.

When I saw this theme in my journal and wrote out the overarching prayer, I realized that God was calling *me* to put feet to it for her. Rebekah had returned to the Lord, and yet her life still had a purpose. Her story would help other young women like Rebekah; but it also would help young men who were in trouble as well as parents and others who have prayed these prayers for their loved one or even lost that loved one in a tragic event.

It was up to me to share her story, yes, but it would also be *my* story of the faithfulness of God and His loving care, even in the midst of unspeakable tragedy and loss.

I do not mean to make it sound like I was fine with Rebekah's murder. I certainly do not want to give the impression that my agony lessened in any way. To do so would be an outright lie. I still flailed in the deep, dark pit of grief. I still found myself barely able or completely unable to do the simplest of tasks.

I did not go to the grocery store alone for over a year. Why the grocery store? I have absolutely no idea, but every time I entered one, I found myself dissolving in sobs. Neither could I wrap my brain around how to straighten up the house. David would take me to one surface or area that needed to be organized. Once I did so, he would gently lead me to the next spot that needed straightening. Making phone calls became a source of great anxiety; for the first time in my life, I transposed numbers. It would take me four or five tries to get the right number punched in the phone. We could be anywhere when sudden sorrow would overwhelm me, and we would have to go back home. The stress of grief wreaked havoc on my digestive system, and I lost a lot of weight over the next year and a half.

As I would go about life as best as I was able, I was certain that anyone looking at me would know that my child had been murdered. I even asked Renee that very question one day when we were out. She replied that she was sure people could see that I was very, very sad.

No, the grief in no way eased. However, I had an anchor to hold in the midst of it: God had not abandoned Rebekah! He had not refused to listen to or answer my prayers on her behalf. She was forever with Him. And He was still with me. What would I have done without this hope? In all honesty, I cannot see how I could have survived. Even knowing this—even clinging to this certain hope—I believed I would eventually die from the grief I felt buried beneath. To be quite honest, that was okay with me. I did not want to be in this world of pain and sorrow anymore.

But this I did know: God *always* hears the cries of His children. And God would be my source of strength and grace to get through this. And, until I did die, I was determined to tell as many people as possible about Rebekah, about the things the Lord was teaching me, and about His faithfulness and tender care.

"All the dreams and hopes you had for Rebekah seem cut short — but the fullness of all the things you wanted for her will be seen — when you are reunited."

Pastor Brandon

9.

REGRETS

2007–2008

As is typical for parents of teenagers, we were on an emotional roller coaster for a year and a half. Rebekah traveled from one bad relationship to another, making some good choices followed by some bad ones, living away from home and then returning. I would be distraught over her poor choices, pleading with God to remove this person or that thing from her life. I would rejoice when positive changes prevailed, then fall back into despair and ugliness when she made poor choices yet again.

I remember my birthday one year; we had no idea where Rebekah was living. She called me that day, talking incessantly and frantically, asking me to affirm repeatedly that she deserved to be treated with respect and dignity. In retrospect, I realize that she was almost certainly high on something. She never mentioned my birthday but told me she loved me, and I promised my love for her.

Later, she apologized for missing my birthday. I told her, "Oh, but you called me that day!" Her response was to say that she hadn't known it was my birthday when she called. I told her it was okay. God had known it was my birthday and how much I needed a call from her.

At one point, Rebekah was arrested and taken to jail overnight for driving under the influence of drugs. She was living with her boyfriend at the time, and we did not know about this incident until a friend in the legal system told us. It proved to be a turning point in Rebekah's life. To the best of my knowledge, she never used drugs again, with the possible exception of marijuana, but I'm not sure she even did that.

She later told me that she had been crying and very upset in that jail cell. A kind guard brought her a Bible at her request. We also learned that the arresting officer said she was a completely different person when she showed up at the hearing, obviously clean and sober.

As a result of this charge, she lost her license and had to perform community service, which she did at the Salvation Army. She worked with a charming woman there who loved Jesus and was so friendly and fun to be with. This woman was truly a bright spot during this difficult time, and she told me repeatedly how respectful, sweet, and thoughtful Rebekah was.

Rebekah enrolled in some classes at our local community college, and our thirty-minute drives there and back were cherished times. About the same time, a family in our church who had horses enlisted Rebekah's help with them. She loved that! And once again, driving her there was a blessing for me.

We had some genuinely good times during the months that Rebekah lived nearby. I would take her out to eat, and we had her over for dinner. We went shopping, and we looked at scrapbooks together (something she had done with me in the years past). And we talked on the phone; I was always delighted to answer the phone and hear Rebekah exclaim, "Momma!"

The family had a celebration for my birthday one year, at which Rebekah gave me a little ceramic tile that said "More Like Mom Every Day" and a Willow Tree figurine. She and her sister-in-law, Jennifer, had gone shopping together. She also bought me an adorable scarecrow decoration to hang on the door.

But there were terribly tough times as well. Rebekah would be doing so well, and then she would be drawn back into dark places. And it was in the dark places where I failed greatly. I failed to see Rebekah for the delightful, beautiful, hurting, precious daughter that she was and instead focused on her behavior. I still did not know how to handle a rebellious child. I took the easy yet destructive way out: withdrawing or trying to force Rebekah to do what I knew was best. Her living at home became unbearable for both of us.

I cannot write what follows without agonizing pain and sorrow in my heart and tears flowing down my face. It would be months later—while she was living at home, drinking, doing drugs, and turning into someone who did not resemble our Rebekah—that I did and said such ugly things. Although I know I am forgiven by God *and* Rebekah (who gave me her forgiveness before she died), I grieve beyond measure.

We tried desperately to get Rebekah help and to distance her from bad influences. Every offer we made—which I cannot remember all of them, but I know Teen Challenge was one—was shot down and rejected. But then I had a marvelous idea that I still believe the Lord could have used greatly. In fact, it may have been her last chance to escape.

We had dear friends who lived in another state and were willing to let Rebekah come to stay with them. She would be able to take college classes, get a job, and be actively involved in their church, which would not judge her. This family had known Rebekah since she was a little girl and would have given her guidelines, which I believe she would have received well, as well as love and opportunities she did not have here.

David and I sat down with Rebekah and told her of this opportunity and how we would be so happy for her to accept this blessing. She listened with a closed-off expression and then said, "You are just trying to get rid of me." At my wits' end, and totally without excuse, I completely lost it. To my great shame and dismay and almost unbearable regret, I left the room sobbing. Like a spoiled child, I grabbed my birthday gifts from Rebekah. I threw the tile that said "More Like Mom Every Day" on the floor, shattering it. I repeatedly threw the Willow Tree figurine until parts of it broke off as well.

Rebekah came upstairs, and with an ugliness I had no idea I possessed, I shrieked, "You are nothing like me! I hate you!"

I cannot tell you how to this day I cringe and grieve those hateful, evil words. I picture them flying like flaming arrows into my Rebekah's already wounded heart. As I allowed Satan to speak through me, I imagine demons dancing and cheering with glee. And I see Jesus, with great agony on His face, trying to comfort Rebekah, even as with unbelievable compassion and unwavering love He looks at me with deep sadness.

Of *all* my multitude of failures and mistakes, I grieve this one to the very depths of my soul. I am struck how when we are frustrated, exhausted, fearful, self-righteous, prideful people, our mouths can easily become instruments of evil rather than love—of utterly ridiculous lies rather than truth.

Of course, I absolutely did not hate my daughter! Never, ever could I have hated her. I loved her and would have given my very life for her at any point in her own life. I wanted to help her, not harm her. I wanted to encourage her, not cut her down. I wanted to be the good mother that she deserved and that I had always longed to be.

But trying to *be* God in many ways—being so passive-aggressive, so judgmental, and yes, feeling alone, hopeless, and exhausted—I sinned. I sinned against God in the way I treated this precious eternal soul He had entrusted to me. I sinned in my thoughts, words, and actions. I sinned against my sweet daughter.

Praise God, Rebekah forgave me. She knew it had been a lie, but it still caused her great pain. I had wounded her soul. Yes, God forgave me too; but I still caused harm that His forgiveness (and hers) does not erase. It's taken me many years to work through the guilt and shame I carried from this as well as many other failures.

Rebekah and I had read a book titled *Bad Girls of the Bible* by Liz Curtis Higgs, who called herself an FBG, or "Former Bad Girl," saved by grace. Rebekah told me she wanted to be like the author and one day, as an FBG, help others struggling to overcome self-destructive patterns. Liz was unbelievably kind to correspond with me through Rebekah's tumultuous years and even past her death. When I shared this most devastating interaction, she told me, "Of course you do not hate Rebekah, but you do hate what she has become."

Such kindness on Liz's part. The problem was that I could not, in that season, see past what she had become to who she really was underneath: *Precious. Delightful. Gifted. Soft-hearted. Kind.* I let her addictive behaviors blind me to the truth that as my daughter, she was still greatly in need of my love. And now that she was grown, it was God's responsibility to correct her and mine to love her as He loves me: unconditionally, unwaveringly, with great affection, and never withdrawing the evidence of that love.

I failed to consistently speak over her the truths of the song by Tenth Avenue North: "You are more than the choices that you've made, / You are more than the sum of your past mistakes, / You are more than the problems you create…"[3] I was good at reminding Rebekah of these truths when she was on the "straight and narrow" again, but my attitude and sometimes my words sadly contradicted these truths too many times.

I did hate what she had become. But what she had become wasn't *her* at all. In rereading my journal entries from that time that reveal my heart for Rebekah, my desire to sincerely love her well and to please God in my handling of difficult situations, I see now that I really hated what *I* had become.

---

[3] Tenth Avenue North, "You Are More," track 3 on *The Light Meets the Dark*, Provident Label Group, 2010.

Rebekah at Peace

10.

ENTERING GRIEF & THE JUSTICE SYSTEM

2009

Having ministered to many people in the midst of grief, I've heard the same mantras from those left behind. A "shattered life" and a "crushed heart" are typical descriptions, and David and I could definitely relate to those emotions.

In addition to seeing my own personal grief counselor, he and I attended an excellent grief support program called GriefShare, which we began within weeks of Rebekah's funeral. Pastor Shane Lilly, of Church on the Hill at the time, led the group, and it was greatly influential in helping us not only survive but also to heal. It was so beneficial that I would go on to lead groups through the program myself in the years ahead.

GriefShare teaches some excellent truths. The first of only two I want to focus on here is that there is no right or wrong way to grieve. We are all different. We have all had unique relationships with the ones we have lost. Men and women tend to grieve very differently. David and I were no exception to this rule, and going through the thirteen-week course helped us from the start to not expect the other to grieve in the same way.

The second teaching is that we must never rank grief. That is to say, we should never look at our own grief and say it is worse than or less than another person's. While this is absolutely true, it is also true that there can be factors that make grief much more complicated. One statistic that really stuck out to us was that it takes three to five years to simply stabilize after the death of a child. Being that Rebekah's death was so traumatic, our family physician compassionately explained that if they were to take an MRI of our brains, it would have looked like we had suffered a severe car accident. The grief caused actual physical injury to our brains. The loss of a child—especially the traumatic loss of a child—would greatly muddle our grief journeys. Added into the mix was that we had to prepare for a trial.

The way it was explained to us was that we could not really focus on our grief. As preparation, we had to exert a lot of thought and energy into everything a trial would entail. I remember that very GriefShare class, listening to a recorded session about how trials greatly entangle the grief process and how they always drag out way longer than expected, making one's grief even more grueling. When I heard that, I remember feeling grateful that the trial for Rebekah's murder would *not* drag out. After all, Ridge never said he didn't kill Rebekah. All the evidence was there, and it was his own father who had called the police. I was certain it would be over quickly.

And I would be wrong.

Ridge said he heard a voice that told him to kill Rebekah. He had also been drinking at the time. To obtain leniency, he seemed to be using the former as a mental disorder defense and the latter intoxication to deny intent, meaning that he did not understand the nature of his actions at the time of the murder. Psychiatric testing was scheduled and then redone. Trial dates were set and then postponed.

Each time a date was set, David and Beth had to arrange time off from work. One of our pastors scheduled around the trial dates as well. I would line up a pet sitter, and Jennifer and Davy would organize childcare. We would try to prepare ourselves emotionally for the facts that would be disclosed and defensively for the media we were sure to encounter. It was extremely draining in every way. And then we would receive notice that the trial was postponed, sometimes with very little notice.

As we went through the postponements, it became clear to us that Ridge had *all* the rights and we had *none*. This was a very difficult truth to deal with. Our victim advocate in Buckhannon, Laura Queen, always listened to our feelings and agreed: it was not fair. But there was nothing we could do. I must admit to feeling angry about what I perceived as a very *unjust* justice system.

Throughout the year and a half that we navigated the legal system, another truth became clear: God had, in His kindness and mercy, in the midst of great evil and loss, provided for us the most extraordinary support system: Laura Queen, victim advocate; Jacob Reger, prosecuting attorney; Doug Loudin, Buckhannon police sergeant, who found Rebekah's body; and the domestic violence organization in Elkins that served Buckannon, Women's Aid in Crisis.

Mr. Reger was very diligent and proactive in pursuing all leads to provide a powerful and effective case against Ridge. While we literally had no say in how the process would go, he was always considerate enough to seek our thoughts and input. When we met in person, he was compassionate and thoughtful. No doubt, he saw Rebekah as someone worth fighting for. We thank the Lord for Mr. Reger, who is now an Upshur County judge.

Sergeant Loudin, now Lieutenant Loudin, was professional to the core and yet full of empathy. He is a gift beyond our ability to ever convey the full magnitude of. The way he handled the case, simply because of his fine character, comforts us to this day. We are beyond grateful for him and pray God's blessings over him and his family. Prisilla Peggs was our contact from the Women's Aid in Crisis organization. She was full of compassion, with an unbelievable desire to help us. This incredible group helped us financially in a variety of ways for which we are still so grateful.

And our beloved victim advocate, Laura. I could write pages upon pages of all this precious woman did for us. She listened to us. She cared for us. She encouraged us. She was so very compassionate, gentle, and kind. She went out of her way to treat Rebekah's memory with dignity and grace and value. She counseled us. She *prayed* for us. Only the Lord knows the mark this woman made upon our lives. She is a dear and treasured friend.

11.

BRIDGES MENDED & HEARTS JOINED

2008

In June of 2008, Rebekah moved to Buckhannon, West Virginia. She was living with a young man and his father in their trailer. When she left, things were very strained between us. But God began to work in my heart. As I look back at my journaling from that time, my prayers were as much for the Lord to change and help me as they were for Him to do the same for Rebekah. I realized that I desperately needed to reveal my love for her—*to* her—in no uncertain terms.

That summer, I attended a scrapbooking retreat. I took a small paper album and wrote the lyrics of a song by Plumb, "In My Arms,"[4] throughout the pages to accompany photographs of Rebekah and me. It is amazing how

---

[4] Plumb, "In My Arms," track 3 on *Blink*, Curb Records, Inc., 2007.

the words of the song describe my Rebekah so perfectly: "curly cues" and "baby blues" and "contagious smile" fit Rebekah to a tee! The part about fairytales and storybooks, queens and kings and blue skies—oh, how Rebekah loved happy endings! I pasted a picture of her as a little girl riding the carousel at Disney World and Cinderella's castle on those pages.

It also speaks of the disturbances to come: clouds, storms, rain. I think of the loss of her grandparents, her illnesses and surgeries, her other struggles. . . . My heart was indeed torn over all these storms in my precious Rebekah's life. I wondered if she still believed in happy-ever-afters.

Oh, how I wanted Rebekah to be safe in my arms . . . to protect and shield her . . . to hold her close and make everything be okay.

I mailed this little scrapbook to her, along with a letter of apology for all that I did that was wrong and hurtful. I told her how much I loved her and always would.

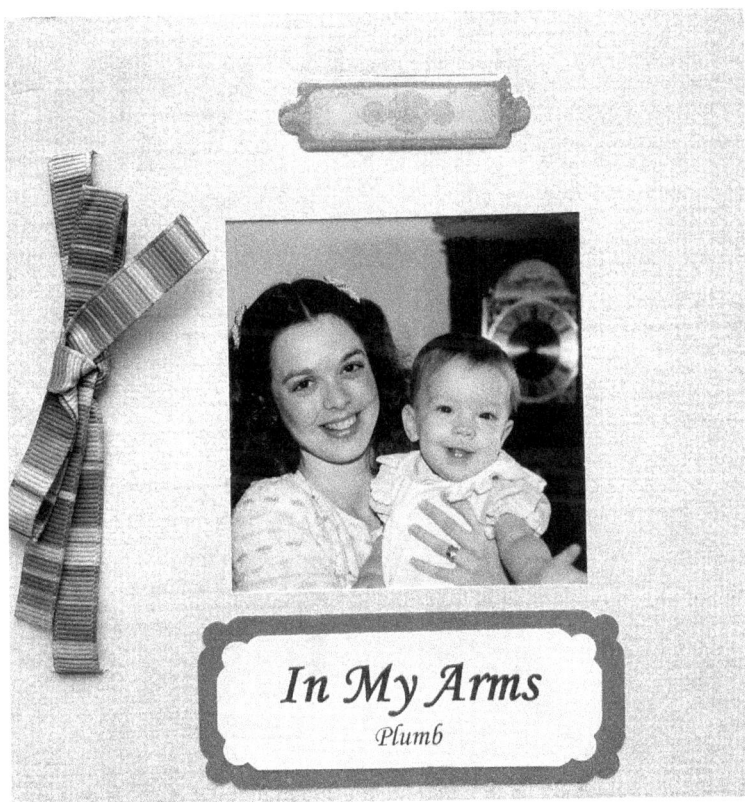

In My Arms
Plumb

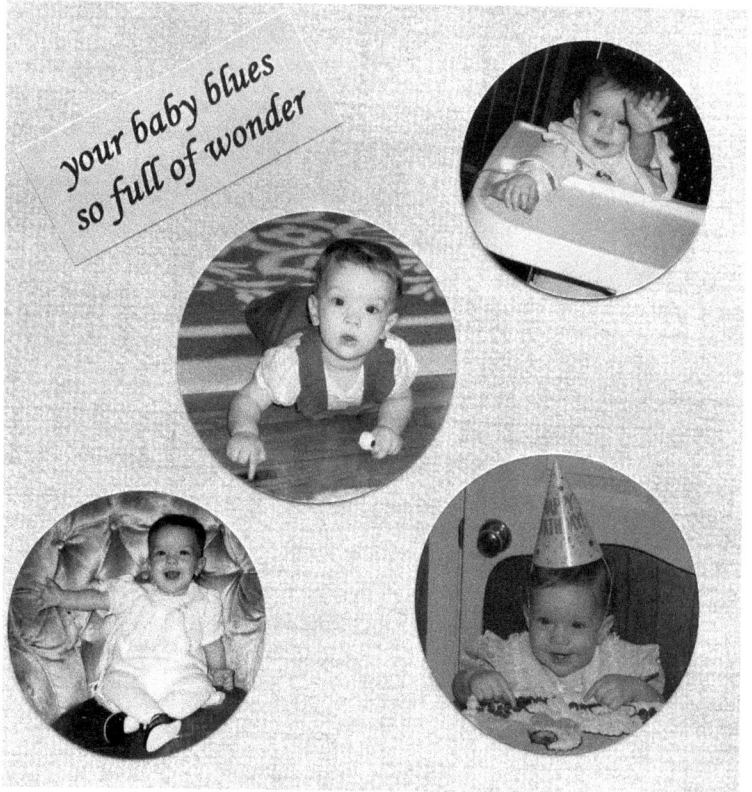

your baby blues
so full of wonder

your curley cues

your contagious smile

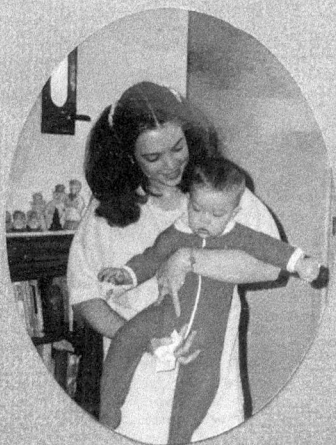

and as I watch
you start to grow up
all I can do is hold you tight

knowing clouds will rage and
storms will race in
but you will be safe in my arms

rains will pour down
waves will crash all around
but you will be safe in my arms

story books are full of fairy tales of kings and queens and the bluest skies

my heart is torn just in knowing
you'll someday see the truth from lies

Castles, they might crumble
Dreams may not come true
But you are never all alone
'cause I will always
always love you

Communication between us became much more frequent. She would call, beginning each phone conversation almost always with "Momma!" We would chat as she shared about her day. She also wrote notes addressed to "Mommy," with the return address, "Your Favorite Daughter."

Rebekah got a job at a local nursing home. She loved the workers there, and they were so good to her. One woman in particular took her under her wing, encouraging Rebekah to leave what had become another abusive relationship. Rebekah set a record at the nursing home for being the new hire to transition most quickly to a full-time employee. Her work ethic was strong in every job she undertook.

Rebekah would tell me stories of her experiences there. In one, she had been assigned to kitchen duty, and if I remember correctly, she burned an entire pan of hash-browns (or something similar) and then dropped them onto the floor. The kind lady in charge said something along the lines of "I don't think the kitchen is the best place for you, honey."

Her job at the nursing home gave David and me the opportunity to love on her by providing some practical support. I had the best time picking out scrubs to send her. One set was a pretty flower print, but my favorites were the Scooby Doo scrubs (we both loved Scooby and watched every episode available) and the set with little snowmen on it—her favorites as well. Having no driver's license, transportation was an issue. So we fixed up her bike from home with a basket and head and tail lights for safety. When her grandmother went to visit Rebekah, we sent the bike and some of my homemade bread. She was so appreciative, and I know it made her feel loved and valued.

In August, David and I were able to take our own trip to visit her. When we arrived at the trailer, she ran out and literally jumped into her daddy's arms, wrapped her legs around him, and clung to him. Healing was happening in their daddy-daughter relationship as well. (I believe this is the image David has of his arrival in heaven: being met by our beautiful daughter and her jumping into his arms.) I got a big hug as well.

She proudly showed off the trailer she was living in, and after we gave her the few items from home she had asked for, including her Bible, we headed out. We took her shopping for groceries, really stocking her and her boyfriend (Ridge's brother) up. There was a little card/crafts shop she wanted me to see in town. We went in and made a card together, and I bought two stamps and a multicolored ink pad. She was thrilled that I enjoyed the shop. We treated her to dinner out, and she was so appreciative of everything.

With my birthday approaching, she had purchased some bath products and a little necklace for me. She also gave me a card that I will treasure forever, which said

I was a good mother—*a good mother!*—who loved and served. She thanked me for loving her. She thanked me again for the little scrapbook, telling me through tears that she was sorry for all she had put me through. I set the birthday card out every August for years after her death. It always invoked tears, but it was also an assurance that even with all my failures, my beloved daughter knew I loved her! It is now displayed in one of the scrapbooks I made of her life, and it continues to bring tears to my eyes every time I read it.

In November, we made another trip to Buckhannon, this time staying overnight in a local hotel. These two days will always be cherished in my heart with deep gratitude. We brought her all kinds of things she had asked for, including some special Christmas decorations in anticipation of the holiday. We took her to the laundromat, and while her clothes washed and dried, she and I sorted through my recipe box, which she had asked me to bring, and copied the recipes she wanted. We talked and laughed and had the best time.

That evening, I gave her a "spa" with all my products from becoming a consultant for a cosmetics and skincare company. I deeply treasure this time of pampering my daughter: of giving her a facial and complimenting her beauty; of gently massaging her hands, arms, and feet; of reassuring her when her scars from cutting were revealed. She expressed sorrow and regret for that, and I promised her it was all in the past. It was a blessed opportunity to

love her in a most tangible way. We took her to dinner that
night and to breakfast the next day.

It was clear that Rebekah was not happy where she
was, and she was missing home. When the time came for
us to leave, she cried. Our daughter did not want us to
go. . . . How deeply this touches me to this day.

In an email to my prayer-warrior friends, I wrote:

We all had the best time! We left with [Rebekah]
crying because we were going back home. But we had a
good plan in place. She was doing so well that we wanted her to look for a job while she was home for Christmas and told her she could stay with us until she got
her feet back on the ground financially. As David and
I drove home, enjoying the beauty all around us, I was
full of gratitude and eager anticipation for Christmas!

12.

FORGIVENESS

February 2009

I had always had a difficult time forgiving others. This should come as no surprise after all that I have revealed in these pages. Forgiveness requires grace and mercy. Forgiveness requires great trust that God will take care of righting wrongs and that He will do all this *without* my help.

Had I ever been asked if I could forgive someone who murdered one of my loved ones, I would have said, "Absolutely not!" And yet, I can honestly say that I forgave Ridge. I did not hate him.

How? How in the world did this happen? I do not have an answer within myself, although I will share some important truths about forgiveness that I think most of us do not understand. But before I go there, I must tell the truth: God gave me forgiveness for Ridge. God quite literally did in my heart what I could have *never* done myself. I am astounded to this day. I see it as one of the biggest miracles I have ever heard of or experienced, and I am filled with gratitude.

What is even more remarkable is that God gave me compassion for Ridge. And—while it is not natural, it is not normal, and I can't explain it or understand it—God gave me *love* for Ridge. The kind of love that grieved an eighteen-year-old who took a life and ruined his own life as well. The kind of love that cringed when people said he deserved to be raped or killed in prison, and the kind of love that prayed for his protection against such evil things. The kind of love that wanted Ridge to come to know Jesus as his Savior and Lord and still prays for this to be true if he has not yet done so.

So, let's talk about what forgiveness is and what it is not, beginning with the latter.[5]

Forgiveness is not saying, "It's okay," "It's no big deal," "Don't worry about it." I could have never spoken those words to Ridge. It was not okay, and it never would be. It was an astronomically big deal. And I certainly hope he will always regret it.

Forgiveness does not mean there should be no consequences. In a situation like this, there absolutely should be

---

[5] I highly recommend the book *Forgiveness,* by Rodney Hogue, which covers these points in greater detail while still being an easy read.

consequences! We desired consequences that would both recognize the horror of what Ridge did and honor the life that he stole from Rebekah. We also prayed for consequences that would keep Ridge from ever hurting anyone else. We wanted justice, and that is in line with a God who is perfectly just. Working within the law to see justice done is in accord with what is right and good in God's eyes.

Forgiveness does not mean we must trust again. Although this doesn't apply to our situation with Ridge, it is important to remember when great wrong is done—even if the wrongdoing is by a loved one. So often, the precious ladies I ministered to in jail would say that their parents had not forgiven them of their past mistakes. They would cite such evidence as not being allowed to move back home, being questioned, and being held accountable. I would encourage them to see the difference between forgiveness and trust: Forgiveness is not being bitter toward someone for their mistakes or injuries they have caused, whether emotional, physical, financial, and so on. It is not allowing hatred and bitterness to grow to the extent that we wish them harm. This has nothing to do with trust. Trust is believing someone will be responsible, reliable, truthful, and upright. Forgiveness is freely given, but trust must be earned.

I will share as a real-life example a business person who lied and cheated us in a variety of ways. They took advantage of our trust, and so nothing was documented or legally binding. It took us years to work through the anger and bitterness we had toward them, but I can honestly say that we came to the point where we did not hate them. We did not wish them ill; we did not dwell on the wrong they had done. We had indeed forgiven them, and yet, we will never do business with them again for the simple fact that we cannot trust them. Forgiveness is a command from God to those who follow Him—trusting someone is not.

Forgiveness also does not mean that we must continue a relationship. This was a truth I shared again and again when addressing those who, like Rebekah, were caught up in abusive relationships. An abuser so often accuses the abused of unforgiveness if they do not welcome them back with open arms. Forgiveness, once again, is not being vengeful or filled with hatred but rather trusting God to see justice done. But even if we forgive our abuser, we always have the God-given freedom to walk away from that abusive relationship.

Then, what in the world *is* forgiveness? Forgiveness is trusting the Lord to take care of the one who wronged us. Forgiveness for me looks like this: While praying for legal justice to be done—for Ridge to be found guilty and sentenced to life—also seeing him through eyes of compassion. It means that I pray for Ridge's safety while in prison. It means that I pray for his soul. It means that I pray for his family. It means that I grieve not only Rebekah's life but also his. It means that I take into account the little I know of his very traumatic childhood. It means

I do all these things by the grace God has given me, for I could not have done them on my own.

Unforgiveness, on the other hand, allows the one who hurt us to steal even more from us. It gives them power over us, whereas forgiveness sets *us* free! Ridge had taken Rebekah's life; we determined that we would not allow him to also steal our peace. We would not waste time and energy focused on hatred or a desire for revenge. We would, instead, leave Ridge in God's hands to take care of in His time and in His way.

Were there times this forgiveness was tested? Absolutely. The hardest was when we were told we might not be able to see Rebekah because of the damage he inflicted in his jealous rage. It was not easy to see him as anything more than a monster at that point.

Is forgiveness easy? No, and I will share more about this later. But I want to share one truth that impacted me greatly and has caused me to thank God again and again for the supernatural ability He gave me, and David as well, to forgive Ridge: Unforgiveness prevents healing. Unforgiveness worsens our pain. Unforgiveness poisons every good thing in our lives and relationships.

I have seen this reality manifested many times over when leading GriefShare, after speaking engagements, or in biblical counseling. In all the years of GriefShare, including the classes that I led, there was only one group of people who made no progress in their grief journey—who stayed stuck in pain and misery: those who refused to forgive. Those who refused to forgive the one(s) who caused the death of their loved one. Those who refused to forgive their loved one—or the one they should have had a loving relationship with but because of abuse, abandonment, rejection, et cetera, they did not. Those who, believe it or not, refused to forgive themselves. And most of all, those who blamed God for the death of their loved one. Those who saw from their perspective a lack of love or power on God's part as a reason to harbor hatred and resentment toward God Himself.

Those who refuse to forgive stay stuck in grief, period.

13.

A Foreboding

November 27, 2008–January 28, 2009

By December, as we were planning for Rebekah to come home, I became concerned about a new acquaintance. His name was Ridge Huffman, the brother of the man Rebekah was living with in the trailer. At eighteen years old, Ridge was barely a man. He lived with a foster family in our area but had gone to Buckhannon for Thanksgiving, where he met Rebekah. And while she spoke of him in glowing terms, I sensed in her a shifting away from the Lord.

On December 6, I journaled:

Father, my heart is troubled over Rebekah. I do not know what, if anything, is wrong, but I have a foreboding feeling. Help me trust You. Help me respond in a way pleasing to You—if there *is* something wrong—and in a way that assures Rebekah of my unconditional, immeasurable love for her.

We did not know exactly when Rebekah was coming home, and she worked hard to surprise me by showing up unexpectedly in my kitchen on December 15. Ridge had driven her to our house from West Virginia. After hugging and loving all over Rebekah, I hugged him and thanked him for bringing our daughter home. David and I had planned to go get her, and it was truly a blessing to not have to make the journey, especially since long car trips caused David's knee to act up.

I had so many plans for the perfect Christmas—for enjoying and helping Rebekah. I made reservations for her, my mom, and me to attend a special tea in Harrisonburg. I was eager for Rebekah to attend our new church and get involved with others her age. I wanted her to experience Church on the Hill and hear its messages of grace and mercy for all. I was thrilled for her to spend time with little Taylor, who was then three and a half and loved her "Auntie Bek-Bek." I assumed she would be home for dinners and games and other family activities.

Once again, Rebekah openly shared her grief over her past choices and how she despaired of any good, Christian man ever wanting her. I tried to encourage her. I told her about Teresa Sours, a wonderful counselor I'd come to know, and I was hopeful she would meet with her.

I had a precious friend, a tad younger than Rebekah, and we three had the best time playing a game together. But as the game came to an end, Ridge showed up and Rebekah dashed off with him. It soon became clear that my "perfect Christmas" would not be the reality. She was a no-show at dinners and came home at all hours of the night or not at all. When she did come home, she would sleep in until late in the morning. She was not the helpful, happy, family-oriented Rebekah she used to be.

On the day of our tea, she had not come home at all the night before. As the time grew closer for us to leave and she still wasn't home, I called and canceled our reservation. I was devastated, deeply hurt, and disappointed. My mom suggested she and I go to Cracker Barrell instead, and we did.

We had barely sat down at our table when Rebekah called my cell phone, wondering where I was and what had happened to our tea. I told her that I thought she wasn't coming so I canceled it. While I held our table, Mom left and picked Rebekah up from our house, which was less than two miles from the restaurant.

Although it had been four years since my daddy's death, Christmas was still a difficult season. I missed him, and my grief became fresh again. Between missing Daddy and being so upset over *my* plans falling apart, I cried through the whole meal. I could barely swallow bites of my food. I was miserable and made Rebekah miserable as well. I failed to enjoy having her there at all.

As meals were missed and nights spent elsewhere, I fell into a place of bitter disappointment and frustration. While I desperately wanted to respond in kindness and gentleness so she could see that I had changed and that my love for her was not dependent upon her actions, my hurt caused me to withdraw again and again. Once more, I allowed Rebekah's choices to hide my precious, hurting daughter from me. And worse, I was once again blind to how judgmental, critical, unkind, unloving, and ungodly my own behavior was.

Rebekah did go to our church's Christmas Eve service, and it was there that she met Pastor Brandon. In the short interaction he had with Rebekah, Pastor Brandon said it was clear to him that she knew Jesus but that she was struggling with her choices. His compassion and discernment comfort me to this day.

On Christmas Day, Rebekah was late waking up, thus missing our traditional breakfast. She did get up in time for opening presents, but my attitude was not the best. As she opened the gifts I had so carefully and lovingly purchased and wrapped, I was not filled with joy. I was distant, which belied the very love those gifts represented.

This was our last Christmas with our beautiful Rebekah. Yes, she played a part in the less-than-ideal situation with her lack of respect and thoughtlessness. But oh, what I would not give to somehow go back and walk through those weeks with grace, mercy, and *evident* love, in spite of my hurt and disappointment.

After all, Rebekah was an adult! I still had not grasped the truth that once our children are grown, it is our responsibility to love them (giving help, insight, and direction when asked) and God's responsibility to correct them. He does so with complete wisdom and the perfect balance of justice and mercy. He, the Bible says, looks upon the heart, not just the actions. His correction is wrapped in unconditional, perfect, unwavering love and is never meted out in anger. He does not pull away from us when we need Him the most.

When I look back through my journals from these weeks, I described Rebekah as being selfish and thoughtless and having not changed at all. Re-reading my harsh words . . . the pain is still almost unbearable. I am also struck by how many times I wrote that Rebekah had not changed, while being so blinded to the fact that I had not changed either.

Or perhaps there is a deeper truth here: Rebekah *had* changed, and so had I; but we reverted once back together, finding ourselves again in our own individual pits of besetting sin (the areas where we were weakest). It is the enemy of our souls that screams, "You have not changed!" The enemy brings hopelessness and despair, covering our eyes, turning our heads away from the loving hands of Jesus, which reach down to lift us out of our pits.

We were making progress; we just had not yet arrived.

Again, I weep, knowing that I am forgiven but ever so sorry for the lack of love that I showed Rebekah when she continued to struggle like I did. My writings are a convoluted mess of self-righteous directions for God to fix Rebekah and my own pleading for forgiveness and His help in changing my heart. Our areas of struggle were simply different. One was no less or more pleasing to God than the other. One was no less harmful than the other.

Rebekah was still so young. She had suffered much in her short lifetime. It is easier for me to understand and empathize with her failures rather than my own. *Now,* that is. Now that my own deception has been removed.

Rebekah moved out and into an apartment with a girl-friend. The last time I saw my daughter was when she came home to gather up her things to take to her new residence. Knowing that cigarette smoke triggered my asthma, she called out, "Stay back, Momma. I smell like smoke."

And I did. I did not hug her. I did not call out to her, "I love you!" I was silent, stewing in my own pain, disappointment, and shattered dreams. I allowed self-centeredness to rob me of my final moments in my daughter's presence. The grief of this rocks me to my core—even today, as I write these words.

Days passed, then weeks. Ridge's foster father came by, concerned that he had not heard from Ridge and fearful that Ridge, and maybe Rebekah, were responsible for some local car vandalism that involved a baseball bat. But I did not call her. I did not reach out to her in any way. I just prayed that an intervention would come in such a way that we could get her the help she needed. I was oblivious to the help *I* needed. And too proud to think that maybe she needed to hear again that I loved her—no matter what.

And then the call from the police in Buckhannon came on the evening of January 27.

14.

SHARING HER STORY

April 2009–December 2009

Having prayed for an opportunity to share Rebekah's
story in a way that would help others like her, I contacted
the women's domestic violence center in a neighboring
city. They agreed to allow me to provide a mini spa service with my skincare products and speak about Rebekah.
Renee was going with me, and some friends gathered to
pray with us beforehand. I was given permission to speak
about my faith, and I prayed that the women would be not
only drawn to the Lord but also wakened to the danger of
remaining in an abusive relationship.

This was my message on April 14:

I would like to share with you the story of my daughter, Rebekah. Rebekah was a beautiful little girl with

blue eyes, brown curls, and a feisty little spirit. She had a family, an extended family, and friends who loved her and provided all her needs as best we could. She was raised in church and accepted Jesus as her Savior at a young age.

At fifteen to sixteen years old, Rebekah started making some bad choices, all of which centered around men. By the time Rebekah was twenty, she had been with at least five different men, all of whom abused her. She was forced to sleep outside on a screened-in porch in cold, snowy weather. She had been thrown out of a car, miles from any source of help. She had been verbally abused, called every bad name in the book, and told she was so damaged that no man would ever want her. She had lit cigarettes thrown at her. She was sleep-deprived by constant banging on doors and walls at night. She was raped and forced to do sexual acts against her will. She was beaten and kicked. She had her nose broken.

This is the little I know of. I'm sure there is more, and I have no doubt many of you have been through worse. One of the men introduced her to cigarettes, alcohol, and drugs.

Rebekah was so very unhappy and would leave a horrible situation for a while, seeking God's will for her life, just to return right back to it or something/someone worse. As her parents, we tried getting her into school—she dropped out; getting her a job—she didn't cooperate; taking her back home—she was disrespectful

and unkind and made our home life miserable. We finally felt we could not take her home again, as we were not
helping her but enabling her to continue with drugs and
alcohol.

We didn't quit though! We offered to let her live
with two different families in other states who were
willing to take her in, away from the bad influences, and
help with schooling and a job. We also tried to get her
to go to Teen Challenge, but she refused them all.

Last May, she headed to West Virginia. Although
she was with another abuser, she managed to get away
from drugs and alcohol, get a steady job, start attending
church, and begin to have hope for her future. While she
was in West Virginia, a lot of the rift in our relationship
was healed. We made two trips to see her, and I even
got to "spa" her, as I did with you all today. This was
the Rebekah we knew: bright-eyed, clean, creative, fun
to be with, great sense of humor, loving, hard-working.
She spoke of coming back home to be closer to all of
her family—especially *me!*—and her little three-and-a-
half-year-old niece. She wanted to get involved in the
wonderful church we had begun attending and find a
good man one day. We saw her in November, and she
was doing well, looking forward to coming home for
Christmas, and maybe for good.

By the time she came home, two weeks before
Christmas, another man had come on the scene, and
with him, he brought alcohol and, we are pretty sure,

drugs back into Rebekah's life. We met the man twice, and we desperately tried to tell Rebekah that he was not nice, a bad influence, and mixed up in illegal activities. She would not listen to us, and our hearts were broken again as we saw her attitude and desires change right before our eyes.

She left our home shortly after Christmas, going back and forth from him to other people, asking them to take her in so she could get away from him.

Rebekah ended up going back to West Virginia with this man, who, in the early hours of January 28, smashed a bottle over her head and then slit her throat

Our beautiful daughter is dead. Our little girl, who assured me she had learned from her past and could take care of herself, had been brutally murdered by an abusive man.

Oh, dear ladies, my heart's cry is that you will re-member Rebekah's story and that because of her death, you will choose to never allow any man to abuse you in any way but stay away from these men, not falling prey to their promises of love and to do better. Rebekah came to this very place but returned to abuse, and now she is dead.

You deserve better, just as she did.

. . .

We honestly had a hard time understanding why Rebekah was making the choices she was, and there were times we handled things poorly. But we always loved her and told her God loved her. Rebekah had a difficult time believing God could really love and totally forgive her, and I believe this is why she had such a hard time breaking free from old patterns. She didn't think she was good enough for God or for a good man.

Ladies, there is nothing God will not forgive, and He loves each of you and has a good plan for your life. If anyone has led you to believe otherwise, they are wrong! The thing is, you must seek Him and follow Him in order for Him to be able to bless you. But whether you follow God or not, and no matter what poor choices or mistakes you have made, no one has the right to abuse you in any way or treat you disrespectfully.

. . .

I believe with all my heart that in God's mercy and grace, He set Rebekah free, and she is now with Him.

Thank you for listening to Rebekah's story. I pray you will take it to heart and walk in safety and the knowledge that you are precious, made in God's image, and worthy of respect and kindness.

I then prayed for and with the women, giving out daisies as a remembrance. It brought such joy and peace and purpose to my hurting heart to minister to these vulnerable women during my own season of vulnerability and grief.

We did it again later, but when we came the third time, in October, the new woman in charge pulled me aside and told me I could not talk about God. I explained how I had done it before, but she said that the staff member who allowed it was no longer there. Renee and I pampered the women as before, and I told what I could of Rebekah's story, but we left feeling empty. Renee heard two of the women say that they had no hope, and it broke our hearts because we were not allowed to share Hope with them!

My mother suggested I contact the Christian Law Association (CLA) about this censorship. One of the attorneys there sent me information that cites specific laws that do in fact allow me, as an outsider, to share my beliefs. I left a voicemail for the director of the center, asking if she would meet with Renee and me to discuss. While waiting for a response, we prayed for God to make a way. It seemed like we kept getting put off, until we eventually learned that the director had taken a leave of absence and we would have to talk to someone else.

When that meeting finally happened, the office manager did most of the talking, albeit in a harsh and condescending way. She said she was a paralegal and inserted herself into our meeting so that the acting director uttered at most a few sentences!

The office manager read the first bit of information from CLA and immediately accused me of misleading the attorney by failing to mention that they are a HUD[6] organization. I told her that I had not known that was the case and was not misleading anyone. But the lecture continued.

[6] U.S. Department of Housing and Urban Development

Because they received federal funding, they could not offer the women any religious information unless they asked.

"Would you give them my name and number if they ask?" I offered. She replied that they could only hand out a phonebook listing of area churches.

Then she said that if, by the time they got there, the women didn't know God, then He wasn't doing His job. If I really wanted Rebekah's death to count for something, she said, then I would start a school for young children who had been kicked out of public schools for poor behavior and had nowhere else to go. She did offer to work alongside me on this. But if I said anything she didn't agree with, she would say "Hallelujah" with a sneer and walk away.

Renee and I had been there for an hour and left feeling like we had been in a battle zone, in which we were the targets! I also left knowing I could never support anything that this woman had a hand in. Renee and I were grateful that we now knew where they stood and that the office manager's ugliness hadn't caused us to act unkindly or disrespectfully or misrepresent the Lord. All I could do was pray for another opportunity to share Rebekah's story where lives would be changed as a result.

Although I was ready to "shake the dust off my feet," I was prompted to check again with the attorney at Christian Law, who sent this:

In fact, the legal rule for a HUD facility is exactly the opposite of what this staff member has told you. Because HUD is a government facility, privately sponsored religious meetings (or in your case, a private citizen presentation) must be allowed in the common area meeting rooms or programs on the same basis as secular private meetings or testimonies are allowed.

It was a violation of First Amendment rights to deny me the opportunity to speak.

The attorney asked me to share this information with the women's center. I definitely did not have the stamina to address the woman who had berated us, telling us that all the women there would go back to their abusive situations no matter what I said. And I did not want to continue to go if they didn't want me there. But I did contact the executive director, and eventually, we spoke on the phone. I learned that the staff member who had first invited us there in April was dismissed for doing so—she "made a really big mistake in allowing you and Renee to come to the shelter," the director said. The bottom line was that they were not at all interested in hearing about guests' legal rights to talk about their God.

When I hung up, I felt so discouraged, until I realized that I had been looking at this situation all wrong. When I first brought up the idea of going there to share, I was told I would most likely not be allowed to talk about my faith. But God miraculously intervened and gave us the opportunity to go, not just once but twice, and talk freely about the Lord and His love for the women there. I thanked the Lord for that opportunity and prayed for the staff member who was let go—for His sake. And I wouldn't quit asking Him to, in His perfect timing, open the door for us to share Rebekah's story in a way that would bring Him much glory.

15.

JUSTICE

August 2009–March 2010

December 9, 2009, was now the date set for trial.

While God supernaturally enabled me to forgive Ridge, justice remained a deep desire. As I read the Psalms and other books in the Bible, I highlighted every verse that spoke of justice being done. I prayed for justice diligently and passionately. I was consumed with the ache for justice.

I was gratified to read Isaiah 30:18: "For the Lord is a God of justice; blessed are all those who wait for Him." I felt the Lord was assuring me that He would see justice done but also that I simply needed to wait on Him. Verse 15 of the same chapter says, "In returning and rest you shall be saved; in quietness and trust shall be your strength."

One day, as I was in the safe haven of my living room couch, which had become the place where I talked with and listened to the Lord, I was reading *Come Away My Beloved*, by Frances J. Roberts. The book said that those in heaven join us as we pray for others here on Earth. It thrilled my soul to think of Rebekah praying along with me, and so I asked, "Lord, would you please tell Rebekah to pray for justice to be done?"

I can't help but shake my head and smile because of God's patience with me.

Question: What is the definition of a controlling mother?

Answer: One who asks God to tell her child what to do when she is in heaven!

And here was another indicator of my pride: that I would *tell* God to do anything! (At least I did say "please"!) While I have never heard God's audible voice, I have certainly heard His Holy Spirit speaking inside of me. His voice is always gentle, and yet He often says what I don't really want to hear. He always seems to take me by surprise, revealing something I have never thought of. His words to me this day fit every one of these criteria.

This is what I clearly heard the Holy Spirit say: *"Nancy Jo, Rebekah is perfectly happy and content to see justice done in My way and in My time. What is most important now is that you are a good witness for Me."*

Wow! A totally new concept: Rebekah was not concerned about justice being done *at all*. She was perfectly happy and content, knowing justice would be served but in God's way and timing. Can I just say that this was one of the most freeing truths I encountered in those months after Rebekah's murder?

The Lord revealed some other truths to me. To place my trust and hope for justice in a jury made up of imperfect people, a human judge, and an incredibly broken justice system was a prescription for disaster. Even if these people and the system worked perfectly, earthly "justice" would never bring healing to my heart. No matter the sentence placed upon Ridge, Rebekah was gone from our lives here on Earth . . . forever. "Justice" could not fix that! "Justice" had no power to bring wholeness to our shattered hearts and lives.

I found in my journals where I had written, "What is most important: justice—limited and completely unable to restore Rebekah's life, here and now—or Ridge's eternal soul?"

I am so grateful that the Lord spoke and revealed these truths to me. Did it change my perspective? Absolutely. Did it mean I did not care about what happened in the trial? Absolutely not. God is just—perfectly just—and it is not wrong to desire and fight for justice here on Earth. The key was that as we continued to pray for justice, as we appreciated our prosecuting attorney's efforts, as I worked on the victim impact statement I would read to the jury, I

was able to do so without that all-consuming desperation
for a ruling that would be just.

> I do pray for justice, Lord. You are just and that is Your
> will. But I leave how justice is attained in Your hands. I
> do pray for the jury, Lord; open their eyes to the truth;
> confound the enemy's every attempt to deceive or twist.
> I pray for our prosecutor; may he think and speak clear-
> ly, Lord. Rest Your hand upon him. And I pray for the
> judge; may his will be aligned with Yours, Lord God.
>
> Most importantly, Father, may Your love, Your
> peace, Your grace and mercy, power and strength be
> so evident in David and myself that You (alone) will
> receive much honor and glory and people will be drawn
> to You. Even the press, Lord. Even the defense attorney,
> Lord. Especially Ridge and his family, Father God. . . .
>
> There is much work to be done between now and
> December 9. I find it interesting that the Lord is just
> now revealing all this to me. . . . Perhaps He had to wait
> until I was ready to listen, and this is why the trial
> was delayed.

We heard that Ridge passed the psych evaluation with "flying colors" and was deemed "perfectly able to stand trial."

We were looking at a court date of December 9 and were told it was unlikely to be changed.

I called Laura Queen, our advocate with the prosecuting attorney's office. She very kindly took the time to answer all my questions and let me know not to expect a plea bargain at this point. The trial would begin on December 9, with jury selection the day before. While we would be in town for the trial, she would work with us to write our statements. Sentencing would occur at a later date, at which time we could give our statements.

Laura said she would try to line up two opportunities for me to meet and provide spa services: one with the ladies who worked with Rebekah at the nursing home and the other with the residents at a local shelter for abused women. Doing this would help get my mind off myself, give me something constructive to do during times of waiting, and give me something positive to look forward to (and back on).

The Holy Spirit made six impressions known to me about the trial:

1. We would be entering a true battleground, where Satan would have his warriors strategically positioned.
2. We needed to be much in prayer and immersed in the Word until then in preparation for battle.
3. We needed prayer support from others, not only during the trial but also as we spiritually prepared for it.

4. I would fast one day a week up until trial, making that day one of focused, intense prayer and remembrance of where my strength comes from.
5. When I focused on justice, I was focusing on the temporal. My focus needed to be on the *eternal*.
6. My heart needed to reflect the Lord's heart toward every person involved—this included Ridge, his attorney, the jury, and the press. I needed to be full of the Holy Spirit so that my flesh did not rise up toward anyone— no matter what was said, no matter what the outcome.

Even embracing these new, freeing concepts, even walking in forgiveness and—what I hesitate to write because it seems so utterly preposterous and impossible and because it could be seen as a betrayal of Rebekah—a genuine compassion and love for Ridge, there was one person I felt hatred for. There was one person for whom I found no grace and could not reconcile myself with their actions and motives: the defense attorney.

In November, Laura called to let us know that the trial would now be scheduled for some time in March. "I realize this is the last thing you wanted to hear today," she apologized.

Just when I felt like I was making real progress in my attitude toward the defense attorney, he decided to schedule a last-minute psych evaluation of Ridge, thus delaying the trial. He said that the first evaluation was biased because the psychiatrist was given the details of the murder; the new psychiatrist would have no knowledge of the crime or why Ridge was being evaluated. If Laura hadn't been looking out on our behalf, we wouldn't have known of the postponement until a few days before the supposed trial date.

I just didn't get it—how was this allowed? It all seemed so unfair, and I was on the verge of tears. I realized I would have to go through all the emotional and logistical preparation all over again. The anger—*loathing* would be a more honest word—I felt for the defense attorney overwhelmed me.

I had expected to use the December trial as an excuse not to "do" Christmas. After all, who would expect me to shop, cook, decorate, et al., in the midst of a hearing? I just wanted it to be over and done with! Now, I had to face the coming holidays and four more months of waiting.

As 2009 rolled into 2010, we were close (I thought), or at least making progress toward going to trial, when Mr. Reger, the prosecuting attorney, was informed by a guard at the Tygart Valley Regional Jail about an inmate who was willing to share some incriminating things Ridge had said and to testify against him. Apparently, Ridge had taken advice from other inmates about what to say to help his case and obtain leniency. The problem was that the informant, along with Ridge, was also a client of the court-appointed defense attorney. In late February, we spent an hour on the phone with Mr. Reger and Laura, who explained that this was a conflict of interest, and Ridge's defense should be handed to a new attorney.

After hearing Mr. Reger's argument, David and I understood. If the judge also agreed, Ridge's attorney would be removed, and a new defense attorney would take his place. This meant that the new trial date of March 22 was out the window.

With this delay, we did find so much to be thankful for: that the guard contacted Mr. Reger, that the inmate was willing to testify against Ridge, and that Mr. Reger was diligent in his work for justice. We were grateful for Laura and Mr. Reger keeping us in the loop and that in this instance, the judge ruled in *our* favor, removing Ridge's attorney and assigning a new one. But besides that, there was no new date, no new progress, and no idea of whether the trial would continue to be postponed.

After the initial blow of yet another delay, I felt at peace about it. I could see how every time the trial had been continued, the Lord drew me deeper into Him, pulling me closer and fine-tuning my focus. I did have a hard time comprehending—accepting and believing—that I was not totally at the mercy of the justice system. It was true that the system didn't seem very just, that I didn't seem to have any control over it, and that those in control didn't seem to consider the impact it had on us. And yet, somehow, I knew that God was in control and that He would work all things to my good.

But as dates for the trial continued to change and more and more requests came in—for further mental evaluation, for permission to use Rebekah's past against her, for more time to construct a defense for Ridge—my anger against the former defense attorney transferred to this new one and snowballed. While my family kept saying, "Nancy Jo, he is just doing his job," I could not reconcile how anyone could possibly defend Ridge.

Ridge had admitted he killed Rebekah, period. There was no need to prove he did or build a case against him. If he were mentally unstable, I thought, that was all the more reason to keep him where he could not harm anyone else. How could Rebekah's past mistakes bring any relevance *whatsoever* to her being brutally murdered? I saw the defense attorney's actions as excusing, or at least downplaying, the horrific murder of my beloved child. And I seethed with anger and resentment toward this unknown person.

We were also concerned about the media. I knew from past experience that the media cannot be trusted to write only facts and to refrain from embellishing or twisting the truth. I can honestly say that I never read any news reports of Rebekah's murder. But I can also say that our friends and family were furious about what was written and broadcast in the local media. David and our sisters shielded me from the pernicious reporting, but many were talking about it.

I actually confronted the editor of our local paper. I told him how hurtful it was to know his publication was spreading rumors about Rebekah that had nothing to do with what happened to her and in no way justified it. He listened sympathetically but said that the paper merely reprinted what was sent from West Virginia. He offered to interview us for a story that would encourage young people to make better choices and help other parents of troubled youth. David and I had no peace about it, however, and respectfully declined, asking instead that he consider more carefully what he chose to print.

(Years later, in 2016, a reporter for another local newspaper offered to share Rebekah's story to bring awareness of domestic violence, and this time we agreed. The writer was appalled at the untrue components of earlier reports and set the record straight, focusing on Rebekah as a victim of domestic violence and the effect of her murder on our family. I have not read this account, but I am told that it is respectful, compassionate, and true.)

We knew we did not want to speak to any media at the trial, but I was fearful of encountering aggressive and disrespectful reporters. I had nightmares about being cornered by them. This was another stressor for me as we prepared to go to trial, and then prepared again, and again, and again. The new date was August 3.

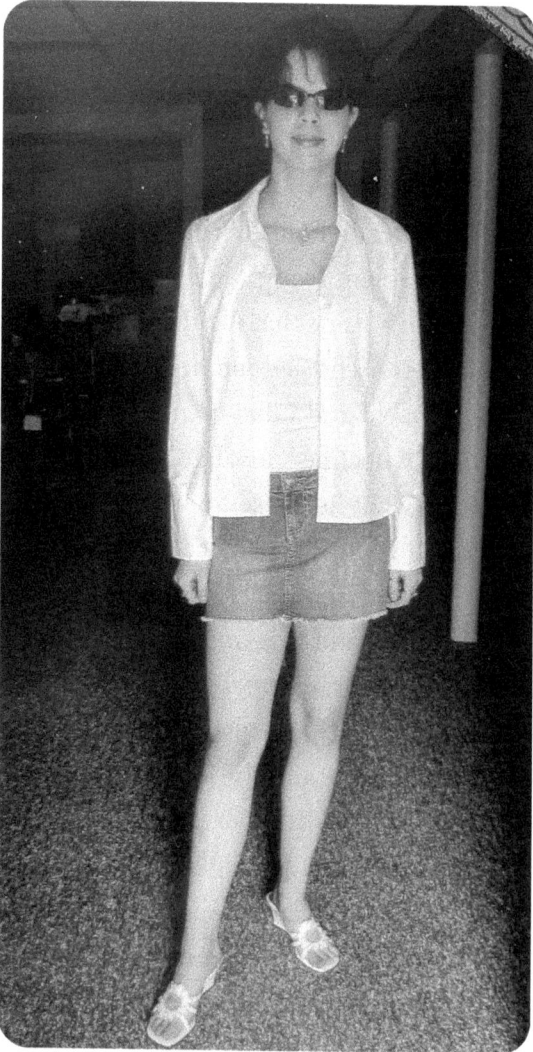

16.

QUESTIONS

March 30–31, 2010

I contacted Laura, our advocate, with some questions I'd
had about conflicting stories. Ridge had broken a liquor
bottle over Rebekah's head, and I'd thought he used the
broken glass to kill her. This was what the police had told
Joseph, and they never corrected the misconception. (After
the call from Ridge's brother on the morning of the murder, Joseph had called the police department to confirm
what he had been told.)

> Dear Nancy Jo,
>   I will do my best to answer your questions. I nor-
> mally do not share your emails with anyone other than
> to let Mr. Reger know we communicate. I let him know

what questions you have that I may need his input to answer. I hope you don't mind that I decided to share your latest email with him. Only because, believe it or not, I don't know every detail of the case. There is a lot I do know and must keep here in this office due to the fact that it is not prudent to put too much out there for others to know.

As I try to answer your questions, I have spoken with Mr. Reger this morning at length to make sure I am giving correct information and still maintaining the integrity of the case. Believe me when I say, I (we) are in no way trying to keep anything from you. . . .

I can tell you there was a knife found, and it is believed to have been what was used. Rebekah did have what is believed to be defensive-type wounds on her arms, and she was struck in the head. There was a broken whiskey bottle found, and Rebekah did have a very high alcohol content in her system.

As to the events of the evening and early morning hours. . . . There was a call made to 911 about a disturbance between a couple, which led to police trying to locate the car described. They were gone by the time police arrived, thus ending up in a phone call to you for details about Ridge's car. Walmart here in Buckhannon is now a twenty-four-hour store—I am not sure that it was then. And to answer how no one could have seen or heard anything—it is possible if the store was not open at that time of the morning.

As Mr. Reger said to me this morning, there was no one there with Ridge and Rebekah when all this was happening, which makes it impossible to answer your concerns about what exactly Rebekah went through or was aware of happening. These are questions that may never truly get answered.

If I could begin to take away your pain with an answer to these and other questions, I would. I can only say at this point, please continue to let me know when you have questions or need to put your fears and pain down in any way. . . .

Mr. Reger wanted me to assure you that we will sit down with you before the trial to prepare you as much as possible for what will be coming out in court. We are not anticipating a request for continuation (I am praying for none), however, the date for any pretrial motions on either part (State or Defense) is July 30, 2010. As always, I will continue to be in contact with any change in the status of the case.

Your opportunity to address Ridge will be at Sentencing, when you make your statement to the Judge and the Court. My suggestion for addressing Ridge is to be putting it down on paper right now—anything that comes to you that you feel you need to say. Journal it, from now until trial. Let your pen talk to him, yell at him. . . . It can be therapeutic in some ways and may make it easier to face him in the Courtroom.

Praying extra,

Laura

Rebekah had defensive wounds. . . . Before this email from Laura, who was so gentle with my bruised heart, I'd thought she had been asleep and unaware of what was happening to her. This was extremely difficult to learn and brought a whole new depth of grief and horror to my soul, as fresh and overwhelming as the day we found out Rebekah was murdered.

Laura explained that by all the accounts and evidence they had at the time, the police had told Joseph what appeared to have happened. After the autopsy and further investigation, they now surmised a knife to be the murder weapon, but Laura mercifully refrained from sharing other details. She also let me know that the police have a protocol for informing the families of victims in a sensitive and timely manner, but that Ridge's brother had jumped the gun.

I was actually thankful it was a knife. It horrified me to think of Rebekah being killed with a broken whiskey bottle. I prayed that the facts would speak loudly to the jury that Ridge had used one weapon (the bottle) to knock her unconscious (I pray this is true—it is what we were told) and another (the knife) to kill her. I am still unable to fathom so much hatred and evil against anyone, especially my own child.

I was inconsolable. My precious sons rallied to my side, as did Renee and my grief counselor. I pretty much shut down and grieved the loss of my child all over again. I spent time in my journal, pouring out my heart to the

Lord and trying to play my "thank You" game, when I think of everything I can to thank the Lord for in a difficult situation. (Believe it or not, I came up with seven thank Yous.)

The other distressing news was that we would not know until July 30 whether the trial would begin on August 3, as scheduled. We would have only three days' notice if the trial would proceed as planned, which seemed to me inexcusable.

Laura warned me that the State and the Defense would have opening statements and facts would be brought forth to set the tone for the trial. If I were in the courtroom, I would be subject to that as well as all the evidence and testimony that would follow. This would include photographs, autopsy findings, and witness testimonies. She said they had some forewarning and control to allow me time to escape the courtroom before such exhibitions, but she couldn't guarantee the same leeway when the Defense presented its case.

Would I come into contact with the defense attorney? If so, the Lord would have to give me grace, especially if he were to attack Rebekah.

With this information, I felt I had taken a huge step backward in my grieving, but each day after was a little better. I felt fear about the trial. I did not want to see photos or hear graphic details of the murder, nor did I want to be present if the defense attorney ran Rebekah's character into the ground or implied that she was partly to blame for being murdered by Ridge. Would it be possible to be in the courtroom and avoid this?

I did, however, in the case of the trial going forward, wish for the opportunity to speak to Ridge's father face to face. I wanted to thank him for calling the police. I wanted to thank him for being kind to Rebekah when she lived with him. I wanted to tell him how very sorry I was for the anguish he was going through. I wanted to tell him that I did not hate Ridge and that I would continue to pray for his salvation. I felt that I should be afforded this one right. Our attorney preferred I wait until after the trial but otherwise did not discourage me.

My heart is breaking
     as I remember how it used to be:
I walked among the crowds of worshipers,
     leading a great procession to the house of God,
singing for joy and giving thanks
     amid the sound of a great celebration!

Why am I discouraged?
Why is my heart so sad?
I will put my hope in God!
I will praise Him again—
my Savior and my God!

Now I am deeply discouraged,
but I will remember You. . . .
I hear the tumult of the raging seas
as Your waves and surging tides sweep over me.
But each day the Lord pours His unfailing love upon me,
and through each night I sing His songs,
praying to God who gives me life.

"O God my rock," I cry,
"why have You forgotten me?
Why must I wander around in grief,
oppressed by my enemies?"
Their taunts break my bones.
They scoff, "Where is this God of yours?"

Why am I discouraged?
Why is my heart so sad?
I will put my hope in God!
I will praise him again—
my Savior and my God![7]

[7] Psalm 42:4–11 (NLT)

My journal entry from March 31, 2010:

"My heart is breaking as I remember how it used to be," both as I miss Rebekah and think of her so very, very often and as I think about what happened to her. . . . I am so sad to know Rebekah was aware she was in danger—I am discouraged to be so deeply in distress and grief again. None of this new information changes all God's words to me: that Rebekah is with Him and is perfectly at peace, happy, and content; that God lifted her up to Him in His mercy and grace; that I will praise Him for all He has done for Rebekah and for me. What happened—what I know and what I will never know—has no impact on my hope in God! Yes, I am very discouraged. But I will remember God—His faithfulness, His promises, His love, His compassion, His loving attention to every detail in my life—and I will completely depend upon Him to get me through this setback.

17.

FEAR & TORMENT

March–April 2010

Six months until the trial. I knew the Lord was in control, and I was trusting Him to work between now and then, but I was tired. August seemed like such a long way off, and even so, we had no guarantees that the trial wouldn't be continued again.

To be honest, I was discouraged. I had the feeling that the trial would never be held, that this would never end, and that we would be left hanging for who knew how long. Of course, these were feelings, not facts, but they *felt* real nonetheless.

David and I were seeing a counselor together, as the stress and strain of our loss and the ever-impending trial on an already rocky marriage was causing great havoc. My counselor encouraged me to record my feelings. Here is what I wrote:

How do I feel. . . ?

I feel sad and lonely: Missing Rebekah more than I can put into words.

So grieved that her life ended at all and even more so that it ended the way it did. I feel unable to truly grasp the idea—the truth—that she is gone, period. I will never, as long as I live on this earth: see her, talk with her, laugh with her, love on her, nurture or nurse her, see her beautiful face, hold her in my arms, or do anything together. The loss is staggering and overwhelming.

I feel afraid: Afraid of what the trial holds for me and those I love. Afraid I will never be "normal" again or even securely reach the "new normal" stage, whatever that is. Afraid heaven won't give me the opportunity to be Rebekah's mommy—to do the things I have longed to do and will never be able to do here on Earth. Afraid the nightmares and horrible images will never go away. Afraid the trial will pull me way down. . . . It is so hard to push my way back up again.

I feel tired: Tired of grieving. Tired of being behind in everything: housework, business, yard work, laundry, etc. I am physically tired too! And tired of being tired.

I feel frustrated: Frustrated with the horribly unjust "justice" system. Frustrated with my inability to think clearly, remember anything, or motivate myself. Frustrated with lack of organization in the house.

I feel anxious: Anxious about my children. Anxious about Taylor going to school. Anxious about keeping my business going. Anxious about being a good sister/friend to so many the Lord has blessed me with—concerned about being a "taker."

I feel overwhelmed: Overwhelmed when I keep the girls, and they both need me, not being able to enjoy and give either one my undivided attention. Overwhelmed with grief over Rebekah. Concern over so many things . . . daily life. Overwhelmed with the stuff I need to do.

I feel angry: Angry with the "justice system": that I have no rights, that they have treated us so unfairly. Angry that any human being would defend Ridge's murder of Rebekah. Angry that the media is so bloodthirsty. Angry that Ridge killed my baby girl, my beautiful daughter. Angry that I didn't do SOMETHING different to prevent this from happening. Angry over things that happened in Rebekah's, Davy's, and Joseph's childhood that I did not fix. Angry with my husband. O Lord, I am full of anger.

I feel trapped financially. This is also a source of anxiety for me.

I am fearful of someone else I love dying.

I am fearful of being a poor witness for the Lord—in my marriage, in my grief/depression, at the trial.

I feel envious of moms who still have and enjoy their daughters, Lord. I am grateful for Jennifer and Brittany—the Lord has been so good to me. But it's not the same.

My hand hurts. I'll quit for now.

I have to be honest here. It's so easy for me to record in this book the good parts of my grief journey, and even some of the bad. As I look at my journal entries from this time and pick what to share, I find that I am skipping over the most awful aspects and only skimming the depths of my grief. It got much worse.

My counselor also asked me to list all my fears about the upcoming trial. It looked like the new trial date in August would be confirmed, and so my list was lengthy. My assignment also included identifying which fears were control issues and which were trust issues. By recording them, I recognized and released the things I had no control over and needed to place in God's hands, trusting Him to take care of those situations . . . and me. Lastly, I was to apply Bible verses that related directly to my fears.

Finances: [Rebekah's funeral plus many days of David missing work put us in a place of financial instability that we never fully recovered from. We sold, as mentioned, our guns and jewelry straight away. Later, we would sell more jewelry, furniture, and other belongings to try to make ends meet. I am positive that this is more often than not a problem for couples who lose a child, but it is rarely made known.] *Philippians 4:19, 2 Corinthians 9:6–8*

Knowing when to be present in the trial and when not to be: [We knew there would be distressing photographs and testimony shared. David wanted to be in the courtroom for all of it. I did not; I did not think I could bear it.] *Psalm 32:8; James 1:5; Psalm 33:18–19a, 22*

Being scarred for life from seeing or hearing something unexpectedly at trial: [I worried about this for David and Beth as well.] *Psalm 91:11, 34:7*

Behaving in a manner not pleasing to the Lord: [Again, I worried about my own behavior as well as David's.] *Philippians 1:18b–20a, 1:27*

Having the peace of the Lord misconstrued as not caring: *1 Samuel 16:7b, 1 Peter 3:15–16*

Coming face to face with Ridge and feeling hatred or other ungodly feelings/thoughts: [I did not want to lose the supernatural forgiveness and compassion the Lord had given me.] *Galatians 5:16–25, 2 Corinthians 10:3–5*

Not knowing how (or being unable) to support David: *2 Corinthians 1:3–4*

Having to face the defense attorney (my heart is not right toward him): *2 Corinthians 10:3–5, Ephesians 4:30–5:2*

Reacting to the press: What exactly does God want us to do? What will bring Him the most glory? Be silent? Speak? If it is to speak, what do we say? *Matthew 10:19–20* What if the press is aggressive? In my face? What if they lie? *Psalm 27:1–3, 6; Psalm 118:10–17; Philippians 1:27*

Not being able to sleep: *2 Thessalonians 3:16; Exodus 33:14; Matthew 11:28; Psalm 29:11, 4:8*

Responding to the verdict: *Psalm 29:11, 26:6–8; Isaiah 5:16, 14:24–27; Philippians 1:27*

Sinking into deep depression again once the trial is over: *Psalm 71:19–21, 34:18; Philippians 3:12–14; 2 Samuel 22*

Coming face to face with the (full) reality of Rebekah's murder: *Isaiah 26:3–4, 1 Corinthians 15:54–57, 2 Corinthians 5:1–4; 1 Thessalonians 4:14–18*

Being "on display": *Psalm 34:1–8, Philippians 1:27* I want so much for the Lord to be glorified. I want Rebekah to be proud of me. I am fearful of failing to do something I should, or doing something I shouldn't that would interfere with this. *Proverbs 3:3–7*

Not being able to read my statement to Ridge, breaking down while reading it, it having no impact on him, or it making him angry: *Philippians 1:27*

Rebekah being painted by the defense attorney in such a light that she is seen as deserving of or to blame for what happened, as well as my reaction to this: *Philippians 1:27; 2 Corinthians 10:3–5; Isaiah 2:22, 5:20–23*

The jury believing Rebekah was to blame: *Isaiah 8:9–10*

Getting Rebekah's things afterwards: [As much as I wanted some of her things, I was fearful of going through her belongings, possibly finding something up-

setting, and enduring more trauma.] *2 Samuel 22:29–33*
Speaking with Ridge's father and how he may respond,
or not being allowed to: [I wanted to convey that we
did not hold him responsible and that we realized he
was suffering too.]

Being sure the Lord's anointing is upon me and my
words: *Matthew 10:19–20, 2 Corinthians 5:17–21*

Will there be an appeal? Will we have to go through
this again? Will it be postponed again? My heart's
desire is to impact everyone I meet with the love, grace,
and mercy of God the Father through His Son, Jesus
Christ. I want those who come in contact with me to
recognize the Holy Spirit within me and to be drawn
to the Lord. I think one of my fears is that I will fail
because I become angry, defensive, overcome with
grief, etc.

I had a lot of fears that spiraled around the what-ifs.
These same fears merged with the horror of Rebekah's
murder to give me nightmares most nights.

18.

THE WAITING GAME

March–June 2010

As I was reminding myself to be thankful for our attorney's wisdom and effort, we received the very upsetting news that Ridge's dad or brother had either sold or thrown away all of Rebekah's belongings. We were devastated as we had none—not one book, article of clothing, piece of jewelry, or knickknack to remember her by. We had put a lot of effort into fixing up her bicycle, but when the police went to the trailer to get it, it was gone.

David was livid. I was hurt, but my grief paled in comparison to the gratitude I felt for Ridge's dad, who had called the police instead of trying to hide or dispose of Rebekah's body. I had no idea what it must have been like to see the things he saw and to know that his own child had murdered someone. Even in my hurt and anger, I grieved for him and prayed that David would not allow his anger to consume him.

The only piece of evidence I had asked for initially was the scrapbook, which was actually in the vehicle when Rebekah was killed. Our pastor contacted the crime victims support program about it, and Laura had the whole police force looking for it. (The car and all her belongings had been impounded and were considered evidence.) They found it, and I was told it would be mailed to me right away. But later, Laura called to delicately break the news that the prosecution felt it was too important not to use in court. Mr. Reger had looked at that little book more than a hundred times and said it revealed who Rebekah was and how loved she had been. Disappointing as it was, I couldn't help but be in awe that it might be used to bring my daughter's murderer to justice.

Once the trial was over, we would get this and some other things that she'd had in the car with her. In particular, I looked forward to getting a cross-stitch she had been working on (I never received this, and do not remember what it was) and a photo album I had made of her dog Opus. She had been wearing a necklace when she was killed, and she'd had a ring in her pocket. But we would have to wait for these as well. As a consolation, Laura took a bundle of Rebekah's photos that had been with her in the car, wrapped them in pretty tissue paper, and mailed them to us instead.

In the early summer, David and I found in the attic some boxes of Rebekah's things from one of her moves before West Virginia. It was a lot of junk and old toiletries, but there were some pieces of jewelry I was so happy to have. And there was a decorative votive candle holder that had a silver celestial design of a sun and a moon. I smiled because it was so *Rebekah*, and I'd had the joy of buying it for her.

We also found hurtful things that pointed to the destructive lifestyle she had gotten caught in—journals in which she wrote ugly things about me and used foul language. It cut me deeply, but David reminded me that this was not who Rebekah truly was, and it certainly was not who she is now! While much of her writing hurt me— partly because of the anger she expressed toward me and partly because I recognized yet again my own failures—I only wish I had been able to receive one insight earlier . . . before Ridge. I would have benefited greatly, *if* I'd had the self-awareness required.

She wrote: "My mom says I am an angry person. . . . I cover up my hurt with anger so no one can see. . . . She needs to look at her own anger issues. . . ." She was 100 percent right! But I had been too blind and full of myself to see this truth. Upon reading this, I thanked God for His forgiveness as well as Rebekah's. And I asked Him to help me when I see angry people, to look past the anger and ugliness to the hurt underneath.

I wrote to Laura that it seemed this nightmare would never end: "I still struggle so with the waiting game, and I feel like it is a game in some ways. A very cruel game."

I was so down, then I realized: I had been praying for more than a year that justice would be done as far as the Lord allowed. Our attorney was looking out for us and for Rebekah, and here I was complaining about it! Yes, this was discouraging and frustrating, and it made me cry. But it was beneficial to the case against Ridge.

Email from Laura Queen, April 8, 2010:

Please first know (if your grief counselor hasn't told you) that this is a roller coaster you are on as far as moving forwards and backwards at a moment's notice. I know it is of little comfort to hear this, but sometimes we can convince ourselves that we should be past all of this. You have not had closure. The roller coaster is still moving, and you are still on it.

You may have good moments when you feel like the ride should be over soon, and then, *bam!* Another upward swing, downward turn, and all the stomach churning and fear are back right in your face. So many twists and turns and feeling like you are out of control. And you know what? We as a system have kept you on the roller coaster. We are mostly to blame for the continuous ride. I wish an apology would help. It won't, I know. You are right in feeling betrayed by even we who are here to try to protect and uphold your rights as Rebekah's family. However, we get stuck in our own system sometimes. Three days' notice is unconscionable, but in the Court's efforts to give the maximum amount of time for the new attorney to go over the case and be ready with any pretrial motions . . . that is the date that was set. If at all possible, I will let you know anything I can as soon as I can. . . .

I am going to say this first as a mother and then as an advocate: You raised Rebekah to be a loving and caring young lady. To love God and her fellow man and not to hurt anyone. You succeeded in that. Ridge was not raised the same way. You do not have to attend any of the trial if you choose not to—that is your right—but if you decide you want to be there for any of it, I will do my best to take care of you and all of your family throughout all of it.

Laura even offered to ask her pastor and church family to support David and I, and any other family and friends, who would be traveling to Buckhannon for the trial in August.

My journal entry from April 17, 2010:

So incredibly sad that my child is dead. Just writing *dead*—what an ugly word, Lord. How terribly final. How difficult to truly grasp that my precious Rebekah is gone from this earth, and I will never see or hear or touch or laugh or share with her again—*here*, where I am. I say "my child was murdered," "my daughter is in heaven," but I never say or even think, "Rebekah is dead." How is that to say, think, or write those three words is so utterly devastating to me—now—fifteen months later? How can it be true? I say, "We lost our daughter." That's not so bad. If you lose something, you can find it again, right? Yes, I know heaven will allow me to be reunited. That is a comfort and joy, and I am so very grateful. Surely, I would not be able to survive the grief if not having that hope. Even so, I want my daughter with me here, *now*. O Lord, the grief is more than I can bear! I miss Rebekah so very, very much. . . .

19.

CONTINUATION

June–July 2010

My journal entry from June 23, 2010:

Well, Lord, here we are—with the rug pulled out from
under us yet again. In the course of one thirty-minute
conversation, we have gone from being fairly certain the
trial will begin August 3 to the extreme likelihood of
a plea bargain, and if not that, another continuance is
possible.

Father God, if it were not for knowing for a fact
that You are in control, I'm not sure I could function
very well right now. If it were not for Your promises of
justice, I would be inconsolable at the way the "justice"
system here on Earth works.

And even with knowing these things—depending on them, clinging to them—I am still full of so many thoughts and emotions right now: frustration . . . anger at how unfair, unjust the justice system is. How the victims are really of no value or interest at all because it is the guilty—the lawbreaker, the murderer—who has *all* the rights.

I learned that Laura had been praying for a plea bargain from the beginning. This carried a lot of weight with me because I believed Laura was one of God's incredible gifts to us. I knew she loved and followed God and that she knew the case and had experience in the system. Still. . . .

The bargain was a guilty plea in exchange for fifteen years to life. It seemed so totally unfair. No justice for Rebekah or for us and such a light smack on the hand considering what he did, knowing what he was capable of. And he could potentially be back out on the streets in fifteen years.

But I addressed all my objections by remembering: Vengeance is the Lord's. He is ultimately in control. I wrote and said it repeatedly. I did so to consistently remind myself until it became a solid fact—one on which I stood securely—and such a part of me that I would recognize when I moved the tiniest step away from complete trust and toward making and holding tightly to my own plans.

David's sister Beth brought up a good point: Why, if
there was going to be a guilty plea, did we go through
all this preparation for a trial? It was a valid question. I
must admit, though, that the Lord worked greatly in me
through all the preparation. I wanted His will to be done,
and I trusted Him completely. In my humanness, I begged
for no continuance but asked for the grace to accept whatever lay ahead.

If we were to go to trial, there was only the slightest
chance that a jury would find Ridge guilty of first-degree
murder and sentence him to life "without mercy," which
means without parole. There is no death penalty in West
Virginia, and so this is the harshest sentence available.[8]
But the jurors would probably consider his young age and
the fact that he was intoxicated and sentence him to life
"with mercy," which meant he would be eligible for parole
in fifteen years. (Someone indicted for first-degree murder
must serve at least fifteen years, according to West Virginia law.[9]) With a jury trial would come the possibility that
they would find him guilty of second-degree murder or
voluntary manslaughter, which would make him eligible

---

[8] For those who are curious, I am not against the death penalty in crimes
that warrant it, such as those that are premeditated and especially heinous.
Although execution is a form of earthly justice, it does not in any way assuage
the grief of a family whose loved one was the victim of the condemned pris-
oner's crime. It could never bring total closure or healing. Worse, it sets off
a lengthy process of court appeals, which would do nothing but prolong the
family's agony.

[9] West Virginia Code § 62-3-15.

for parole in ten years. Therefore, the plea bargain gave us the verdict that a jury would most likely settle on without us having to endure the torture of a trial.

As June came to a close, we waited to learn if Ridge would accept the plea bargain or not, if the trial would take place or be continued. I found it was a whole lot easier to "trust" the Lord to bring about true justice when I was sure there would be some decent earthly justice too! It seemed like the justice system was merely playing a calculated game of chess, in which we were the helpless—disposable even —pawns.

My thoughts were full of words like *unfair* and *unjust,* but God had been over all this with me before. He had said that justice would be done in His time and in His way and that Rebekah was perfectly content with that. He had told me to be a good witness, which I assumed meant at the trial. But He never specifically said *trial.* He merely said that Rebekah was not concerned about justice in the courtroom and that the most important thing was for us to be good witnesses for Christ, period. God had known all along we would end up here, and He knew now whether there would be a trial or a plea bargain. Although I still didn't know, I did trust that God also knew what was best for me and all involved.

On July 6, the Defense requested a continuation of the trial.

20.

PLEA BARGAIN & SENTENCING

August 2010

For a few weeks, we did not know if there would be a trial or another continuance and, if the former, they would be able to seat a jury. We had regular phone calls from the prosecutor's office to prepare us in the case of a trial. They wanted as few surprises as possible for us, and so we were briefed about what would likely be said.

These calls were extremely tough. We knew Rebekah had made some poor choices. But to know that the Defense's plan was to rationalize her murder—to give the jury the impression that she was a bad person and that Ridge should not be unduly punished for his brutal act. . . . It was crushing, and frankly, it outraged me.

Then, in early August, Ridge accepted the plea bargain and pled guilty to first-degree murder, receiving "life with mercy." He would be eligible for parole in fifteen years.

Laura comforted me on the phone, explaining that it would have taken us a long time to deal with everything we would have seen and heard at a trial. I believed her, and I believed that the Lord had spared us that horror. Still, I was numb, and although I would not have to endure a traumatic trial, the task before me would surely not be a pleasant one.

On Monday, August 9, David and I left our dog Ronald Anne in the capable care of a dear friend and traveled to Buckhannon, along with Beth, arriving early in the evening. Because of the sudden change of plans, not all of our support team was able to make it; this made me feel anxious about being "alone." I wrote to my prayer team, asking them to pray:

> That others—Ridge, his family, the press, whomever—
> WILL SEE WHAT THE LORD HAS DONE AND BE
> AMAZED . . . that they WILL PUT THEIR TRUST
> IN THE LORD.
>
> One last request: that the Lord will work in Ridge's heart so that he will hear what is said. That he will not laugh or scorn us. I can handle hatred and indifference. Laughter or scorn will be very difficult for me to handle

in a godly way, I'm afraid. And I want him to really hear that God loves him and will redeem him, if he will just ask.

I made Psalm 40:1–3 (NLT) my "new song" for the next three days:

> *I waited patiently for the Lord to help me,*
>   *and He turned to me and heard my cry.*
> *He lifted me out of the pit of despair,*
>   *out of the mud and the mire.*
> *He set my feet on solid ground*
>   *and steadied me as I walked along.*
> *He has given me a new song to sing,*
>   *a hymn of praise to our God.*
> *Many will see what He has done and be amazed.*
>   *They will put their trust in the Lord.*

All my anxiety about not being supported was a waste. We were not alone. In fact, we found in Buckhannon a multitude of cherished friends, family, and even strangers, who went out of their way to love, encourage, comfort, and provide for us. From the time we arrived until we left, we were treated with such honor and loving-kindness. We were further touched by the generosity bestowed to us.

Worried about our finances and unable to get a loan at such short notice, we had borrowed money from a family member for lodging, meals, and fuel. It turned out we only had to pay for our gas. The local Women's Aid in Crisis organization provided the hotel rooms and all our meals, except for lunch on Wednesday, which was covered by our church. The Lord met these and every other need abundantly beyond my imagination!

What a joy to receive my long-awaited hug from Laura Queen, who had honestly been one of our most reliable friends during the eighteen months since we lost Rebekah. I had not met her face to face until that Monday evening, and I was overcome with gratitude for all she had done for us. She had been professional, knowledgeable, and organized; she had tended to every detail for us and yet had been so loving and compassionate through it all.

As soon as she had heard about Rebekah, she'd put our family on her church's prayer list. And while writing this book, I learned that Laura had been ready to resign from her position as victim advocate in March 2009. But when she got the call about our daughter that awful January morning, she felt it was God's will to advocate for us, and so she did.

The next day, with Laura as our guide, we visited the prosecuting attorney's office. Mr. Reger was so kind to us. I couldn't help but wonder what it must be like to put hours and hours of time and effort into a case and then not get the chance to present it before a judge and jury. If he were discouraged or disappointed in any way, it was not evident to me. I believe Mr. Reger made justice for Rebekah, as well as what was best for us, his first priority.

Every person in his office treated us with the utmost respect and compassion. It was not a cold, uninterested atmosphere—it was warm and comforting. Every person we were introduced to met our eyes, shook our hands or hugged us, and spoke kind words. Then Laura acquainted us with the courtroom, where the next morning, we would be sworn in and allowed to give our statements.

When we arrived in time for the ten o'clock hearing, Pastor Shane, who had been by our side through all the horrors, was there to pray for us, comfort us, and love us. To our surprise, Davy and Jennifer had made it, and I tearfully told Laura that we had a son and a daughter with us. (Joseph had been in Haiti at the time.) Our neighbor Jamin, who was a pallbearer for Rebekah and who we considered our "third son," also surprised and touched us with his presence. All of these, along with Beth—who never left our side, understood the tremendous pressure we were under (for it affected her too), and even provided much-needed comic relief during the journey—gave us the support we required for the next hour or so. We also had Susan, Renee, Mama, and many others at home, praying around the clock. The Lord heard and answered all our prayers!

We were each able to speak coherently before the judge. When it was my turn, Ridge did not laugh, smirk, or look at me with contempt. He maintained eye contact for the most part, but at times looked down. I have no idea what was going on in his mind, but I prayed that the Lord would speak to his heart and bring to remembrance the things I said. While my voice shook with emotion, tears had to be wiped away, and (much to my embarrassment) I had to stop to blow my nose, my words were clear and able to be heard and understood by all in the courtroom.

Ridge,

Why didn't you drive away and leave Rebekah at Walmart? Why did you have to hit her on the head with a bottle?

Why, when that blow knocked her out and did so much damage, did you then feel the need to further mutilate her by slicing into her beautiful neck?

Why couldn't you have just let her go? Why did you come into her life—take her down your path of destruction—and then kill her?

How could you murder our precious child when you knew how much we loved her? When I hugged you and thanked you for bringing her home to me at Christmas? When you sat and ate dinner at our table and could see how precious, how loved, how treasured she was? When, another time, you watched as she, a friend, and I played a card game and you saw her sense of humor, her gentle spirit, and again, how loved she was by us?

Ridge, I pray you are behind bars for the rest of your life. Even though I realize you will be eligible for parole, it is my prayer that parole will be denied. Because of your choice to brutally murder my child, her life on Earth ended at twenty years of age. I will never get to hug her, laugh with her, watch a movie with her, scrapbook with her, make cards with her, plant flowers with her, go shopping with her, cook with her. I will not be able to help her plan her wedding or hold her child. I will never receive another phone call when she says, "Momma!" I will never receive another note addressed to Mommy.

I have had to listen to my three-and-a-half-year-old granddaughter ask about her Auntie Bek-Bek and the bad man who hurt her feelings and sent her to heaven and if all the bad men are in jail. I have had to watch as she, at four years of age, loves on her baby sister, pats her cheeks, and says, "Now, Callie Jayne, don't you go to heaven without me! We are going as a family."

Thanks to your brutal act of rage, there will never be another day in my life that I do not miss and long for my daughter. There will never be another holiday— from Christmas to Easter to Mother's and Father's Day to Thanksgiving to her birthday and even my birthday—that is not marred by grief. Even looking at my beautiful granddaughters—playing with them, rocking them—even that, which should be 100-percent joy, has deep pangs of grief, for they both remind me so much of Rebekah. And Rebekah, who loved babies so, will never get to see her namesake.

We would be here all day if I tried to share one quarter of the ways your murder of Rebekah has harmed us: emotionally, mentally, physically, and financially. And it has harmed countless others who loved Rebekah and who love us.

Thanks to you, we have seen Rebekah's name dragged through the mud by the media. You have had the opportunity to have your side of the story—which is totally and completely unverifiable, and *never* will be [verified]—paraded in the media, while Rebekah's side of the story has been effectively silenced by you— forever.

Your act was so brutal, so vicious, so destructive, and the damage you inflicted upon Rebekah was so se- vere that we did not know for several days if we would be able to view her body.

Again, I want to be very clear: I pray you will spend the rest of your life in prison for the murder of my daughter, Rebekah. That is right and just and fair—not only for Rebekah and for us, but it also prevents another family from having to endure the suffering we have had to endure and *will* endure for the rest of our lives.

That being said, I do not wish that you go to hell, Ridge. I would not willingly allow Rebekah's mur- der in order for you to go to heaven. Were that in my hands, you would spend eternity in hell. The amazingly wonderful thing is that Almighty God does love you enough that He *did* willingly allow His only Son, Jesus, to be murdered so that you can go to heaven and spend eternity with Him. I cannot begin to fathom such a love! He allowed Jesus to experience—and Jesus willingly endured—such unbelievable, horrific suffering, all so that you, I, our Rebekah, and everyone who will just ask Christ into their heart to forgive them of their sins can go to heaven. You deserve hell, Ridge. And so did Rebekah. And so do I. Rebekah and I made the choice long ago to accept the gift of salvation through Jesus. I pray that you will make that same choice.

For I promise you this: One day, we will all stand before God Himself, Perfect Ruler and Righteous Judge of all. God Almighty, who knows all we have ever done. We will, each one, either be sentenced to hell or allowed into heaven for all of eternity. And Ridge, none of us will have a defense attorney to try to sway the verdict! Jesus's blood alone is what determines our eternal destination. Rebekah's and my sins are washed away because of Jesus. Your sins, even the murder of Rebekah, can be washed away too. I pray you will ask the Lord's forgiveness and that you will truly surrender to Him and obey Him. If you do that, although you may be in prison for the rest of your life, the Lord will be with you to comfort you, guide you, protect you, and even use you to bring glory to Him.

I know this because even in the depths of overwhelming grief and sorrow, He has been faithful to be there for me—to speak to me and comfort me and enable me to survive a grief I would have thought impossible to endure.

I pledge to pray for you, Ridge, until the Lord takes me home and I am reunited with Rebekah. I will pray that you confess your sins to God, that you turn from them, and that, by God's grace and power, you walk in obedience to His Word. I will pray that you, Ridge, as a newborn child of God, will be used to share His gift of salvation with many, many others and that by doing so, you will have a part in taking what Satan intended for evil and allowing God to bring about much good. You will be able to experience true freedom and joy if you surrender to God.

Regardless of whether or not you accept Christ, God does not remove the consequences of our sin. It is my hope and prayer that in choosing to take a life, in choosing to brutally murder a defenseless young woman, your life, at least your freedom, is taken in return—if not forever, at least until you are not a threat to anyone else.

I have no doubt that the Lord held me together for the courtroom, for as soon as we were out of it, I broke down. But I want to mention another prayer that was answered: I was concerned that when I came face to face with Ridge, I would have been overcome with rage or hatred. I was not. I honestly felt grief for him. Not one member of his family was there: no father, no siblings, no aunts or uncles, no grandparents. His foster father from Virginia was there, and that was all. My heart broke for that reason and made me pray that he would turn to his heavenly Father, who will never leave him nor forsake him.

We had said from the beginning that we would not speak to the press, but the Lord had other plans. A television reporter for West Virginia's Channel 5 news approached Laura and asked if we would reconsider making a statement. Since Laura trusted this reporter, we gave a short interview, and although we never saw the result, I pray that the Lord used it in some way.

We were told that when the ugly reports about Rebekah had first been broadcast, the local people agreed she did not deserve that. A police officer who had been in the courtroom later tracked us all over town to tell us how much he appreciated what we had shared at the hearing.

October is Domestic Violence Awareness Month, and the city of Buckhannon wanted to dedicate it to Rebekah. They invited us to attend the Women's Aid in Crisis organization's annual candlelight vigil for victims of domestic violence. It would be held on the Upshur County courthouse steps, and both Laura and I would speak about Rebekah. It would be a touching memorial to Rebekah, and I felt this was another answer to prayer—that her death would not be in vain.

David, Beth, and I all agreed: as stressful as those three days had been, we could not imagine what it would have been like to go through a trial. God was indeed merciful to us. We felt a huge weight lifted off our shoulders and thanked God that the "trial" was behind us. Even so, I knew that our lives would not go back to normal. There would never be a "normal" again.

21.

SERGEANT LOUDIN & THE SCRAPBOOK

August 2010

Sergeant Loudin, who had discovered Rebekah's broken body and stayed with her that morning, was also in charge of her belongings that had been in the car. He had inventoried everything and packed it all into a suitcase, a backpack, and some plastic containers.

When we walked into the police station, he stretched out his arms to me, holding in his hands a little book. On it, I saw the photograph of me holding baby Rebekah and the title, *In My Arms*. It was the scrapbook I had so desperately wanted back. The only way I can describe the scene is to compare it to the gentleness and honor with which a folded flag is handed to a military widow.

With much gratitude, I took the book, and then he hugged me.

I can say for certain that this little album was ordained by God; He gave me the idea and provided the perfect pictures and song lyrics. He used it to bind Rebekah and me together again as Mommy and beloved Daughter. Rebekah treasured it until the day she died—and I know this not only because it was in the vehicle when she was killed. We discovered that she had copied the lyrics into her own journal and titled it, "My Mom's Love Song for Me." She wrote me a letter and said that the song helped her understand my perspective in a deep way:

> One day, Mom, you're going to know how much this means to me. It made me understand and see you in a whole new way. I love you so much. I'm sorry I have hurt you and made you so sad many times. Thank you for always seeing me, even when sometimes I didn't, and no one else did either.

Sergeant Loudin and the chief of police helped us load Rebekah's things into our Yukon, and then we drove home.

I later received a letter from the sergeant (now a lieutenant and still with the Buckhannon police department) tucked inside a lovely card:

Dear Nancy Jo,

I'm sorry I have not written sooner. I have had this card and intentions of sending it to you since the day you stopped by the office to get your daughter's belongings. I guess I never realized how much your Rebekah's passing had affected me. I have wrestled with what to write and how to write this for some time. I wanted so much to tell you while you were here, but I struggle to keep my composure. However, I was told this might give you some peace of mind.

First of all, I'm sorry I could not save your daughter from the horrible violence she received. I was the only city officer on duty that tragic night. I had actually been driving through the Walmart parking lot earlier in the night. I keep asking myself why couldn't I have just driven through, seen what was happening, and stopped the violence before her life was taken? For that, I feel I failed to protect Rebekah. I have failed you because I could not keep your precious daughter safe from harm.

I became a police officer to help people. In this line of work, you become a counselor, teacher, minister, enforcer of rules, and protector of the innocent. I was unable to protect your daughter, and for that, I am deeply sorry. I am frequently called upon to go into the schools and talk to the kids about the dangers of drugs and alcohol and about violence. I tell them that the hardest part of my job is to have to tell family members that their loved one was killed for one reason or another. I talk to victims of domestic violence about getting away from their abusers. But I was unable to be there to help your daughter—to steer her in the right direction—and for that, I am sorry.

I do not go to church as often as I should (mainly due to my work schedule), however, I do have a deep and firmly planted faith in God. This is what I was told that may bring you peace of mind. The day I found your daughter in that car, while I was checking to see if she were still alive, I leaned in and whispered to Rebekah to go in peace and rest easy. I also prayed to God that she did not suffer and that if she were gone, He would take her, love her, and give her a better place than where she had been. I also asked God to be with you when you were notified of her passing.

The day you were here, I wanted to tell you, but I would have lost all composure. For waiting this long to tell you, I'm sorry. Please forgive me. I pray that God gives you peace and strength throughout your life. As a parent myself, I can only imagine your grief. Please know that your daughter was cared for as if she were my own. There is not a day that goes by when I drive by Railroad Avenue and through the Walmart parking lot that I don't think of your daughter and how I wish I could have saved her.

I am amazed at your strength, and if (God forbid) I would ever have to go through what you have been through, [I pray] that I would have an ounce of your strength and resolve to sustain me. I apologize for not being here when you spoke at the domestic violence awareness ceremony. I truly wanted to be there.

I also wanted to tell you that while going through your daughter's journals, I could see Rebekah's love for you and her family. You could tell she missed being home and doing things with you. I could also tell that she felt guilty for where she was at the time and longed to be home so she could go back to the time when she was happiest.

I hope this does not ruin your Thanksgiving festivities. I hope you and your family are well. If you are ever back in Buckhannon, let me know. I would love to see how you are. If there is anything I can do or help you with, let me know.

Yours truly,

Doug Loudin

P.S. Thank you for your kind letter. It was truly inspiring. I can also see where Rebekah learned to write and the joy of reading and writing poetry.

22.

GRIEF REPRISAL & THE DEFENSE ATTORNEY

August–September 2010

Our sisters offered to sort through Rebekah's things to spare us from any deep pain that might cause. Beth hand-delivered the photo album I'd made for Rebekah of her dog Opus, which I had wanted for a long time. Otherwise, David and I couldn't bring ourselves to unpack anything else.

It seemed we were experiencing what we had been told from the beginning were manifestations of the injury done to our brains by the trauma of Rebekah's death. For David, it was panic attacks in social situations and depression; for Beth, fear; for me, transposing numbers, wanting to withdraw from the world, and being on the verge of tears most of the time. We were all having bad dreams. All these symptoms, among others, made it seem like we had taken backward steps in our grief, and it was overwhelming.

One morning, as I lay in bed, crying, I told David, "I want to say to the Lord, 'Father God, I have tried to be obedient to You. I have tried to be a light for You. I have chosen to forgive as You command. I have . . . I have . . . Now, Lord, can I *please* have Rebekah back?'"

David said she would not want to come back, and I agreed that it was extremely selfish of me to even want her back in this old world. But I missed my daughter!

A local reporter called, and I finally gave in. When the article appeared, Beth was worried that someone had leaked one of my private communications, but it wasn't so. I was very forthcoming on the phone, thinking that the more information I gave them, the less chance they would have to say they didn't know the facts. I was outspoken about our lack of trust, and this reporter was quite gracious about it and put me at ease.

Although the Lord was so good to allow me to forgive Ridge and even feel compassion for him, I still struggled with feelings of hatred and bitterness toward the defense attorney. Perhaps by using the word *struggled* I am making it sound better than it was; in all honesty, I really didn't fight these feelings. *To defend a guilty person was wrong. It was not biblical. How dare anyone defend the murderer of my child!* These justifications for my loathing consumed me. I knew it was ugly, but I persisted to view him as the enemy.

While we were in Buckhannon, Laura had pulled me aside. In her gentle way of understanding where I was and not condemning me for it but also wanting to share the truth, she told me some things about the defense attorney. She knew how I felt about him and how I agonized over being in the courtroom with him, had there been a trial. Laura explained how hard it is for defense attorneys in general to face the families of victims in court.

"He's a good man, Nancy Jo," Laura said. When he and his co-counsel left the prosecutor's office after looking at evidence in our case, they were visibly burdened and grieved by the savagery of the crime.

Furthermore, Mr. Reger made it clear that Ridge would have never accepted the plea bargain unless his attorney had urged him to do so. Ridge agreed to the plea bargain at around noon on the Friday before sentencing. The attorney stood with him before the judge about three hours later to make it official. In the time in between, Ridge could have changed his mind, not to mention every time the judge asked him if he were sure of his answer. The stress was so great that the defense attorney had to be taken to the hospital because of the effect on his blood sugar.

These things rolled over and over in my mind after we returned home. One Sunday, about a month later, I had a revelation, which I later wrote about in my journal:

> I was struck anew with awe that the God of the Universe has actually spoken to me. . . . As I contemplated this wonder, I felt impressed upon my heart to write the defense attorney and apologize for my hatred of him leading up to the trial. I said, "Where did that come from, Lord?" Then I said, "You are a rascal!" That may seem irreverent, but I don't mean it that way. It's just that I can see You—watching me, waiting for just the right moment to speak to me that which I do not want to hear, and timing it in such a way that I simply cannot brush it off. And so help me, I think You are smiling! Okay, Lord, I will write him. I trust You will give me the words. . . .

I waited until David and Joseph left to go watch football at Davy's. I knew tackling this letter would be emotionally draining, but I had no idea how much so. I sobbed as I composed what I wanted to say and then again when I rewrote it on stationery. I did not make excuses; I simply shared my honest feelings and asked his forgiveness.

It was humiliating to confess to this man the depths of my undeserved hatred for him. The next day, I scribbled in my journal a complaint to the Lord: "You don't let me get away with anything!" I almost felt like God was picking on

me, holding me to a higher standard than others. I wondered if He asked extra of me or asked me to do things
He didn't ask other people to do. "I would rather focus on
You helping me miraculously forgive and have compassion
for Ridge—the indisputable evidence that You live within me—than admit that my sinful nature is still alive," I
wrote. But then I realized that if I wanted to completely
be free, I had to be obedient, and I hoped that it would also
bless the attorney.

And lo and behold, the pit of grief I had been stuck in,
for the first time ever, seemed not so dark.

23.

RIDGE

November 2010–April 2011

I want to say that if when I say the Lord gave me a motherly type of love for Ridge, you recoil in disbelief, it's okay! I know I would have done the same before I experienced this crazy miracle.

I have shared my thoughts as I sat across from him in the courtroom. I had prayed that he would not smirk at us; I'm not sure how I would have handled that, but I do believe the Lord would have helped me. Ridge, however, never spoke a word. He did look at me respectfully, and Laura said his attorney would have instructed him to do so.

My shock was great when, at the beginning of November, I found a letter from him in our mailbox. In the letter, he asked for our forgiveness again, saying that he knew we had said in the courtroom that we forgave him but that he wanted to ask for our forgiveness personally. He spoke of being afraid, of being sorry, and of praying that Rebekah was safe in heaven.

To reply or not to reply was the question.

I chose to reply, assuring Ridge of our forgiveness but reminding him that *our* forgiveness wasn't really what he needed to worry about but rather God's. I told him that God would absolutely grant forgiveness, *if* Ridge confessed his sins and surrendered to and followed Jesus. I told him that he did not need to pray for Rebekah because she was indeed safe and perfectly happy in heaven. I thanked him for writing to me.

Soon I received another letter in the mail. Against the counsel of several friends (but not all), I began to correspond with Ridge and continued to do so for more than five months. Those who opposed my letter-writing did so out of complete concern for me. They did not want me to suffer, and they did not want me to be taken advantage of. Many questioned Ridge's sincerity. It turned out that they had good reason to.

For me, however, I practiced something my daddy had taught me many years before. I wrote out Ridge's possible motives as well as the possible outcomes of my writing back or not:

Scenario 1—Ridge is not sincere, and I do not write: no one loses.

Scenario 2—Ridge is sincere, and I do not write: I was concerned that this would be a huge loss of opportunity to share the love and truth of Jesus with him, that it might cause him to doubt the sincerity of our words at the sentencing, and that I would be a poor reflection of God's heart for Ridge.

Scenario 3—Ridge is sincere, and I write: big win and best-case scenario.

Scenario 4—Ridge is not sincere, and I write: I might be taken advantage of.

Writing was the only option to my way of thinking. Being taken advantage of was far less concerning than missing an opportunity to put feet to my prayer that Ridge would come to know and follow Jesus. In every letter I sent, I spoke of God's love for Ridge; I answered any questions he asked; and I was brutally honest, saying that he needed to stay in prison to pay for what he did, with the only exception being if he turned his life around with God's help.

Ridge's family seemed to be out of the picture, and I grieved at the thought of him having nothing at Christmas or on his birthday. I sent him some books, each one hand-picked to reveal his value in God's eyes, how much God loved him, and how God could and would help him change if he let Him.

In April, I received a call from the prison. Ridge had asked to meet me, and I told him I would be willing. I suppose he needed permission from the prison authorities and when he asked for it, they were alerted to our correspondence. It was against the rules for an inmate to communicate with the victims of a crime they committed. The woman who spoke with me was very kind, and honestly, for the very first time, I felt like the system was working to protect and help *me*. She said that while I had not known the letter-writing was not allowed, he was well aware.

She asked what Ridge had told me. Did I know that he had been involved in a gang and that, they believed, he still was from within the prison? At her request, I sent her copies of every letter he had sent, as well as copies of my replies. I had kept all our correspondence, just to be on the safe side. After reviewing the letters, she called again and told me that Ridge was absolutely taking advantage of me and not being honest. She pointed out specific things he had asked for that revealed ulterior motives. For instance, he had asked for a photograph of Rebekah; fortunately, I had not granted that request. She said it was not uncommon for gang members to keep "trophies" of their victims.

This all made me ever so sad—but not for myself! I felt and still strongly feel that I did the right thing. I pray that even though Ridge's motives were not right, some of the truths I shared, some of the scriptures, might remain in his mind and one day bring him to repent and follow Jesus.

But it made me sad for Ridge—that he wasn't honest and that he was still under the influence of evil.

I know that a church began a ministry to Ridge, corresponding with and praying for him. I hope they still do.

24.

FREEDOM

May 28, 2022–Today

As hard as it may be to believe, I had indeed forgiven my child's murderer. I had even forgiven the attorney appointed to defend my child's murderer. However, these are miracles that have very little to do with me. Remember, I was not the forgiving type. But those of you who have reached this point in my story may realize that there was still one person I had not yet forgiven.

Ridge killed Rebekah fourteen years ago, and for fourteen years, I have been blaming myself.

This final chapter actually began one year ago, when I started writing this book. I want to address it directly to you—the reader. It's about freedom, and I share it in the hopes that if you (God forbid) have suffered a loss like mine, you would find freedom—not from grief because it will remain, although its intensity may come and go—but freedom from guilt, shame, and regret. Freedom from the past. I pray you will find the grace to accept God's forgiveness and ultimately, to forgive yourself.

A popular saying is "Live life with no regrets!" When I looked it up, I found numerous articles: "11 Ways," "15 Ways," "40 Ways," and so on, "to Live Life with No Regrets." But the truth of the matter, despite what the Internet says, is that there is only one way to live a life with no regrets: *Never do anything wrong! Always make perfect choices!*

Okay! Good luck with that!

To regret is to be very sorry. *Regret* (as a noun) may refer to distressing emotions such as sorrow. Hence, regret is sorrow aroused by circumstances beyond one's power to repair; it is remorse that comes with the understanding that we acted, spoke, or thought in a way that harmed others and/or ourselves and displeased God.

Regret in and of itself is not bad. In fact, I would go so far as to say that if we have no regrets, we should be alarmed. But immersing oneself in sorrow, shame, and condemnation because of those regrets *is* bad.

The Holy Spirit has worked in me for these many years, bringing increasing freedom from guilt and shame for an abundance of sinful words, actions, and attitudes in my past. But in the last year, as I have been writing this manuscript, He has shown me with greater clarity that my regrets have been holding me captive. He has spoken and revealed things to me again and again—because I am a slow learner, and He is an ever-patient Teacher.

This journey has not been easy, and preparing to share it has not been easy either. I have discovered *only* three valid reasons to delve into our past failures—our regrets:

1. to change, so that we do not continue to repeat the same wrongdoing;
2. to help others learn from our mistakes; and
3. to glorify God—to give Him all honor and praise for working in our hearts and lives and helping us become more like Jesus.

The last two reasons are why I am baring my soul on these pages to you who do not know me or Rebekah, at the risk that you may judge her or me as a result. But I do desperately want to learn from my mistakes and share God's goodness with you.

Full freedom from regrets can only come after the very painful process of confronting the ugliness of our sin. In speaking of freedom from regrets, I want to be sure not to convey in any way that our sin is not costly. I don't want any of us to abuse God's grace by excusing, justifying, or minimizing our guilt. We mustn't approach our failure with a flippant attitude—a dismissive "Oops, my bad" or "Sorry, Lord," as we go on our own way with no thought for the pain we have caused Jesus, who suffered for our sin. Sometimes, because God is not right in front of us, because we cannot see the pain we have caused etched on His face, we fail to grasp the severity of our sin.

Not to mention the people we hurt—including ourselves. Even an unintentional mishandling of a situation can cause deep pain, and sometimes I was—and admittedly still am—oblivious to how my accusatory and judgmental ways injure the people I love.

And what of the one I wronged long ago? I cannot tell her again how sorry I am, and she is not here to tell me she forgives me. The only two words that adequately convey my feelings about this are genuine *horror* and *mortification*. I am appalled by what I have done, and I have no defense.

But I have learned that God does not want us locked in a room of regret. His forgiveness is prompt and complete. He does not want us to dwell on it or beat ourselves up over it.

The journey I am sharing here begins with these excruciating lessons, though I didn't recognize them as such years ago. Obviously, I don't walk these lessons out perfectly. Old habits die hard. But as John Newton said, "I am not what I *ought* to be; I am not what I *want* to be; I am not what I *hope* to be in another world; but *still* I am *not* what I once used to be, and by the *grace* of God I am what I am."

The great majority of my regrets come from my failures as a mother. Even as grief continues to swell from time to time—as we will always miss Rebekah—my feelings of self-condemnation, shame, and regret also rise up with a vengeance. This past year, as I began to write this book about Rebekah, her murder, and the amazing things God has done—the book you now hold in your hands—I have, of course, had to revisit the past. And I won't lie: it has been brutal.

On May 28, 2022, I journaled during my quiet time:

Father God,

I have barely begun my book. I have a box of tissues now by the computer, for as I type, I cry.

Tears of grief awakened.

Tears of longing for the story to have been different.

Tears of gratitude for all You did . . . gratitude for all who were Your hands and feet.

And . . . tears of regret.

These tears flow, mingled with the other tears, even now. I know You have forgiven me. I know my beloved Savior's body was beaten, broken, mutilated, and crucified for *all* my sins. I know Jesus rose from the dead and that I have new, eternal, abundant life in You. I know I am Your child. . . . *But* I don't know how to step away from the tremendous grief of all my failures—my wickedness—Lord. The soul wounds I inflicted upon my precious children . . . my anger, my rejection, my allowing Satan to speak cruel, judgmental, condemning words through me, my too-harsh punishment . . . and not just for the precious children You placed in my arms to love as You love, but for David and hundreds of others I wounded with self-righteousness, judgment, and pride. . . .

The overwhelming grief slumbers for a while, but it is awakened when memories come to the surface. Your Word says in James that we are to weep and grieve over our sin. I've got that down pretty good. But You also say in Romans that we are to be freed from guilt, condemnation, shame. . . .

There should be an end to this grief. I just don't know how to reach the end.

Other than this, I do not know how to express how devastated I was. As I wrote, as I remembered, and as the regret threatened to overtake me, the enemy was quick to jump in and say, "You have not *really* changed." (I am so grateful for the kindness of my husband, who countered, "But, Nancy Jo, you *have* really changed!")

As I continued to work on the book, the end of August found me still floundering:

Lord, as I write my book, my heart breaks over and over again as I relive my utter failures—my ugly, mean behaviors and words—yet again. Yesterday about did me in as I wrote about our last Christmas with Rebekah and the last time I saw her. Sobbing, I felt again the crushing, unbearable weight of my sin. . . . Lord, I know You have set me free and long to increasingly bring more freedom from guilt, shame, and regret . . . and I want to embrace this as my right as Your daughter. But is freedom from sorrow my right?

How do we work through this? I don't know exactly. But I do know how the Lord has gently and patiently helped *me*, giving me an analogy—a series of interconnected visions over a three-month period. I recorded the visions, as they were given to me, in my journal.

The first scene was a room filled with boxes of regrets, piled floor to ceiling, and empty of anything else.

I have a room full of past failures. I opened the door for You [Jesus] to come in and forgive me! I opened the door enough for You to come in and change me! I opened the door enough for You to give me Your humility to own, learn from, and share my failures in the hope of helping others. And yet . . . that room is still crammed full of box after box after box. Some filled with shame, others guilt, lots of boxes of regret, and many boxes of sorrow and tears.

I have been opening the door wider, bit by bit. . . . With Your help, Holy Spirit, I can get that room almost cleaned out! And then something happens . . . memories resurface or a new failure . . . and quick as a wink, there are more boxes in the room!

The second scene: I once again saw myself among my boxes of shame and regret.

Satan was putting boxes on my shoulders, and Jesus was taking them off. The boxes kept coming, faster and faster. I would accept them and set them down in my room; Jesus would pick them up and throw them out. But more came in than were thrown out. . . . Finally, Jesus sat down on one of the boxes and just looked at me. I could feel His eyes upon me. I continued taking boxes and avoiding His gaze. I knew He wanted me to look at Him, but I didn't want to see irritation, aggravation, or a resigned look that said, "I give up!"—a shaking of the head and rolling of the eyes, coupled with a look of disgust.

The Holy Spirit almost forced (yet in a gentle way) me to look at Jesus, and tears were streaming down His face. His gaze was filled with nothing but sorrow and love.

The last scene, as recorded in my journal:

Lord Jesus, I told You I had a question for You about all those boxes. No matter what I do, no matter how You help me, it seems I struggle to clear that room out. The same boxes keep showing up! My question was "Do I need to sit with You and go through the boxes in order to be set free?"

I saw You sitting on a box—no tears on Your face now, just love. I got a box to bring to You. It was so heavy I struggled to move it—dragging and pushing, bit by bit—until it was in front of You.

I knew what was in it: hundreds of photos of my most grievous failures to love my children well. Thousands maybe. I opened it up, and there they were. But there were mouse droppings and dust, and many were stuck together. All the images were distorted.

I climbed up on Your lap and cried as You held me. I know the exercise of asking where You were at specific traumatic times in our lives, but I have resisted that because I didn't want to immerse myself in the ugly reality. I felt I needed to do this, though, and I brought up one of my absolute worst failures to love well.

The memory was one I've already detailed in Chapter 9. It was when we offered Rebekah the opportunity to live for a season with some out-of-state friends, who were willing to help her. Rebekah, who knew and loved this couple, angrily accused us of trying to get rid of her. Instead of walking away or calmly discussing it further, I ran upstairs. I threw the birthday gifts she had given me onto the floor, where they shattered. And when she followed me upstairs, I told her I hated her. Of course, that was a lie, but it was a cruel lie.

The regret over that single incident—the guilt and shame and immense grief—weighs a ton all its own.

> As I allowed myself to see that scene again in the kitchen, it was from Your perspective, watching me. I was hesitant, not wanting to see the demons I'm sure were present, but as I looked, what I saw were wounds on *me*. I know there were many, but what caught and held my complete focus was my heart. It literally hung out of my chest by a bloody cord.

Immediately, the saying "Hurt people hurt people" came to mind. I remembered how full of hope I had been to offer this rescue to Rebekah and how shocked, hurt, and overcome with anger I was when she rejected it. Seeing it again from this perspective, I was impressed by the essential requirement that we run to Jesus with our hurts *before* we react—before we strike back at those we love the most.

I asked my question again: "So what, Lord, do I do with all these boxes of horrific failures?"

Jesus reminded me of my earlier vision in which He simply threw the boxes out of the room. He did not sit down, open each one, and call me over to examine the ugly, jumbled contents. He impressed upon me: *"These boxes were all packaged by Satan. Why in the world would you want to go through them? Remember the mouse droppings? The distorted images?"*

Months earlier, my co-workers at church had prayed for me as I visibly struggled with deep heartache while I wrote this book. One of them prayed against the ways the enemy was deceiving me. A few days later, during my quiet time, I asked the Lord what I was missing. How was I allowing the enemy to deceive me?

This time, I found myself in a little theater, sitting in a typical theater-style chair. I was not tied to it and could have left at any time. In front of me was a large screen, upon which scenes of ugly things I have said and done played out in a loop of living color. When I looked to my right, I saw an old-fashioned motion-picture projector, gleefully operated by a demon who was all too delighted to present reel after reel of my failures on the big screen.

Then my gaze fell to the floor. All around the stand upon which the projector sat, covering the floor inches deep, were scenes of film that had been spliced from my children's childhood. The Lord spoke to my heart, telling me that these reels of film captured the things I had done *right.*

I was not a complete failure. I did love my children! I had taken care of them and had fun with them and sacrificed much for them. I had done . . . the best I knew how to do at that time.

To be honest, while I appreciated what the Lord showed me, it didn't really stick with me until a while later. I was at my dining room table with my editor, Dara, and her mother, Lynne. I wanted them to get to "know" Rebekah, and so I was sharing with them the two huge scrapbooks I had made, beginning with her birth all the way through our last times with her.

While glancing through the many photographs and hearing me tell lots of stories, Lynne commented, "You were a good mother, Nancy Jo!" At that very moment, my mind flew back with crystal clarity to the rolls of spliced film on the floor of the little theater.

Yes, I'd made mistakes—terrible, costly mistakes. Yes, if there were any way to turn the clock back, I would do things differently. But the mistakes and failures were not the sum total of my motherhood. As the Bible says, "Love covers a multitude of sins,"[10] and I cling fast to that promise!

I remembered Pastor Brandon also looking at that first scrapbook and saying, "Nancy Jo, there is no way your children did not know you loved them." After Rebekah's

[10] 1 Peter 4:8 (ESV)

death, Joseph was sitting beside me as I cried on our basement floor. With his arm around me, he said, "Momma, no matter how many mistakes were made in a day, you always held us, rocked us, and sang over us. At the end of the day, we knew you loved us!" Of course, he was talking about when they were little, but it was, nonetheless, a balm to my soul.

We all have regrets—some more devastating than others. Satan desires to crush our spirits by focusing our attention on those exclusively. But do *not* be deceived.

> *You are more than the choices that you've made*
> *You are more than the sum of your past mistakes*
> *You are more than the problems you create[11]*

I printed these lyrics from a song by Tenth Avenue North in Rebekah's second scrapbook, knowing the message was true for her. I had failed to realize then that it was true for me too. It's true for *all* of us!

Back to Jesus's question: Why in the world would I want to go through the boxes Satan crammed full of my failures? Why would I do that when I can trust Jesus to bring only the things He knows I need to examine and only when it's for a very good reason?

And so, I pictured cleaning out the room with Jesus. When it was finished and I was about to close the door,

---

[11] Tenth Avenue North, "You Are More," track 3 on *The Light Meets the Dark*, Provident Label Group, 2010.

the scripture came to mind about a house that is cleared out and swept clean. Jesus said that if the house remains empty, evil will only fill it again, and even worse than before. I thought, "I need to fill that room with boxes of *good* memories—the things I did right and the wonderful times we had." But the Lord quickly spoke. *"No. No boxes at all! Why have a room you cannot use?"*

Good memories and fun times—these would be the pictures on the walls and the colorful knick-knacks on the shelves. The decor, as it were. But the furniture—the sofas, chairs, tables, lights—these would be made of the amazing grace, mercy, forgiveness, and love that Christ Jesus has poured out on me. Not a tomb. Not even a memorial. This would be a room to be *lived in*—a room where I can invite others to enter. Where I can tell them of the goodness of God, where I can extend the same grace and mercy and forgiveness that I have received, and where I can bask in the unconditional love God has for me.

What a beautiful room this will be!

I want this book—this final chapter—to be such a room, full of the redeeming love and forgiveness of God. If you feel burdened by what you have read thus far, this is where I want you to put it down. Give it to Jesus. You have my permission. I do not want anything in it that is disturbing to linger, only the good that God is working out of it. And if you have been accepting your own boxes of guilt, death, ugliness, and pain, here is where you let Jesus throw them out. I'll even help! I'm getting better at it myself.

"But I don't deserve to have my boxes thrown out," you say. That is precisely the beauty of our Savior's love. None of us deserve it. I certainly hope I have adequately conveyed that *I* do not deserve it. This is why it is called *grace*. God gives us the freedom, desire, and power to change— even though we do not deserve it. This is why it is called *mercy*. Instead of the punishment we deserve, God pours out His love and forgiveness.

If you have spent too many hours watching a film edited by demons, you do not have to keep watching. You are free to get up and walk away. There is more to the story than what is being shown on that screen. Why watch a horror movie, in which you are the villain and the victim, when you can star in an epic romance? As you walk down the dark aisle toward the light, you may hear Satan claim, "You don't deserve it." But that's when you lift up your arms in gratitude to the Father who so lavishly gives to His children exactly what we do not deserve! Time to leave that wicked theater for good.

And when you do, I'd like to invite you to come inside this room. There is another side of the story you need to see.

It is full of the light of God's love. Come, take a look at the photographs on the walls. You'll see a darling baby girl with blue eyes and brown curls and a winsome smile. You'll see a little girl in a bathing suit, laid out on the side of the pool, just barely allowing her toes to get wet. You'll see her many beloved pets and cute older brothers. You'll see her horseback riding and piano playing. You'll see a young woman, glamorous and brooding, in a wide-brimmed hat and with a Mona-Lisa grin. You'll see me, chin up in pleasure and affection for my daughter, who has come up behind me to wrap me in a hug.

Jesus and I are still working on this room, but let me point out a couple of highlights. There's the upright piano, gleaming with polish and stocked with new song sheets. Favorite stuffed animals and dolls line the sofa—no longer careworn, but plush, clean, and bright-eyed. The shelves hold books and bundles of cards and envelopes, addressed to "Mommy" on Sunset Drive, "Dear Diary" pages and school papers that exclaim "I HATE MATH!"

I hold out a colorful tile to you; you'll see the cracks are still there, but just barely and only if you look hard for them. "More Like Mom Every Day" it says, and that Mom is trying her best to become more like Jesus every day. The stab of pain it once brought grows less sharp as the cracks become less visible.

Please sit down next to me here, and let me tell you something: I don't always get it right. This is a process. But I am more free than I was. And I want *you* to be too.

Therefore, there is now no condemnation for those who are in Christ Jesus, because through Christ Jesus the law of the Spirit who gives life has set you free from the law of sin and death.

Romans 8:1–2 (NIV)

He does not treat us as our sins deserve
or repay us according to our iniquities [sins].
For as high as the heavens are above the earth,
so great is His love for those who fear Him;
as far as the east is from the west,
so far has He removed our transgressions from us.

Psalm 103:10–12 (NIV)

And I am certain that God, who began the good work within you, will continue His work until it is finally finished on the day when Christ Jesus returns.

Philippians 1:6 (NLT)

EPILOGUE

2023

As I come to the end of writing Rebekah's story, we have passed one milestone and are moving toward another. April 23, 2023, would have been Rebekah's thirty-fifth birthday. On difficult days, I try to arrange something to look forward to—a way to honor Rebekah or bless another, a treat for David and me, or some way to glorify the Lord for all He has done. This year was no different.

Rebekah was famous for how perfectly fine she could crumble and cook ground beef. It was one of those quirky things that she did exceptionally well—much to her dismay because I would always ask *her* to cook it! I literally never cook ground beef or pork and not think of Rebekah. Even my daughter-in-law Jennifer always remembers Rebekah when she cooks ground beef.

One day, I was looking for something on Amazon. I don't remember what it was, but a nifty gadget popped up that helps you cook up finely textured ground beef. It wasn't overly expensive and had great reviews. So I ordered four in black—one for me and one for each of my daughters by marriage: Jennifer, Abby, and Amanda. I kept them stashed away for several months, not even using mine, because I didn't want any of the girls to see it and ruin the surprise.

For the birthday, I made each daughter-in-law a card—black and red, which were Rebekah's favorite colors. In it, I told them how much I loved and appreciated them as daughters and shared the story about Rebekah and ground beef. I then wrapped a red bow around each of the gadgets and set them aside to hand-deliver on that Sunday after church—Rebekah's birthday. I then had something to look forward to.

I always say that I would never choose to bring Rebekah back to this old world when she is with Jesus, David's mom, and my daddy. It has been fourteen years since we have had Rebekah here to celebrate her birthday, and still, the day was overwhelmingly sad for me. I cried all morning. I cried at church. I cried after church. I got teary-eyed presenting the girls with their little gifts and cards, although I tried to hold myself together. I cried that night. I cried the next morning. It was an extremely difficult day. Quite harder than I had expected.

The Rebekah-shaped hole in our hearts is still here. No one and nothing will ever take her place. The completely debilitating grief has subsided, and we have more good days than bad. But grief still surges in agonizing waves from time to time. I struggle to picture what my beautiful twenty-year-old daughter might look like as a thirty-five-year-old woman. I cannot. I long for new pictures, new memories. I long for her presence. This ache that reaches to the depth of my soul will never be eliminated this side of heaven, but our God is good! Rebekah cannot come here to us, but we *will* go to be with her again! And this time, Momma will make no mistakes! I will not fail to love her with perfect love, for I will be totally free of my sin nature. This is my most favorite thing to look forward to!

At the end of the day on the twenty-third, David and I both felt a bit guilty that we had not gone to Rebekah's grave that day. We will before long. But on that day, I shared with David when he brought it up that while I felt the same way, I could hear Rebekah telling us that she is *not* at that grave. She is alive and well! And it gave her pleasure—and maybe even a laugh or two—when we shared those gadgets, cards, and love with the daughters the Lord has blessed us with here on Earth.

On Mother's Day, we attended a National Honor's Society ceremony for our granddaughter Taylor, who was graduating high school. I was completely surprised when they read Taylor's address: "I would like to dedicate all my achievements to Rebekah, who helped my family grow." Such an apt insight! I know I have grown much because of Rebekah, and our family has too—in more ways than one. Today, we are blessed with *six* granddaughters to dote on!

Grief—without the ability to experience it, we could never be like God. We would be stuck in a loveless existence. We have a God who grieves infinitely more than us because He loves infinitely more than us. But how grateful I am that He does not abandon us in our grief, that He sends His Holy Spirit to comfort us, and that He carries and sustains us. He walks with us through the darkest valleys and promises that one day—*one day*—there will be no more death or crying or pain. And we will—together with our loved ones who have loved Jesus and gone before us—be with Him for all eternity. I cannot wait!

January 28, 2024, will mark the fifteenth anniversary of Rebekah's murder. We have been told that the parole hearing for Ridge will occur on that very date, but I have a feeling that is not accurate, as it is a Sunday. When Beth reached out to the parole board to get information and then relayed it to us, I was once again surprised by how it impacted me. We have known this date was coming for thirteen years. But now it is real. And as the saying goes, time goes faster the older we get.

It is close now.

Not only is it close, but again, we are facing many unknowns about how the judicial system will work. What will we see and hear? Will we see Ridge? Will we be allowed to interact with him? What will we be allowed to say? What will be the outcome? Will people be kind? Will Rebekah's memory be held dear?

There are too many factors I do not know to account for. But there are also some things I do know. We will not be alone. Beth will be going with us. Lieutenant Doug Loudin will do everything possible to be there. Perhaps Laura Queen and other family members will be there. Most importantly, God will be there, and again, I hear Him saying to me, *"The most important thing is for you to be a good witness for Me."* That is my heart's deepest desire!

I hope to be able to ask Ridge if he has surrendered to and is following Jesus. I want to again tell him that I have forgiven him but that I believe prison is the best place for him to be, unless a true and deep transformation in his heart and soul has come about through faith in Christ. I hope to adequately convey my love and appreciation for anyone who does show up on Rebekah's and our behalf. I hope parole will be denied. I hope we will not have to relive any past horrors or learn of any new ones. I hope it will not pull us down into the pit of grief again.

I am sure there will be other things I will hope for as the time draws closer.

One winter evening when the children were young (I'm guessing Davy was nine, Joseph seven, and Rebekah five), I had to drive the four of us to church in my husband's truck. We were all squished together in the front row, which was stuck in position for David's six-foot body, which did not suit my five-foot-three frame well. It was raining, and the defroster wasn't working. I was sitting on the edge of the seat, straining to reach the pedals and peering at the dark road through the diminishing spot of clear glass on the windshield.

We had gotten about two-thirds of the way there when Joseph said, "Mommy, my tummy hurts."

"Joseph, I'm sorry your tummy hurts," I responded. "Do you know why it's hurting?"

"No," he said, which was followed by Davy's emphatic "I know why it's hurting! It's because you're afraid!"

What a blow to my ego! My driving wasn't *that* bad.

Joseph countered, "I'm not afraid."

Davy: "Well, you ought to be!"

Joseph: "Well, I'm not!" And just as I was ready to thank him for not doubting me and my driving skills, he continued: "I've already prayed about it, and if we all die, it's God's will."

It seemed neither boy—who had no control over the truck or the situation—had confidence in his mother's abilities to get everyone safely through this danger. And yet Joseph knew he did not have to fear because God was ultimately in charge and had it all under control.

As I said, in the case of this forthcoming parole hearing, I hope for a lot of things. But like Joseph, my hope is in God. God has already proven Himself to be faithful, kind, merciful, gracious, and loving beyond what I could have ever dreamed. I know He will be faithful again. And because I know He is able to work all things together for my good and His glory, I am determined by the power of the Holy Spirit within me to not put my hope in the justice system, to not put my hope in parole being denied. If I can keep my focus on the goodness of God, no matter what, I will walk away from the parole hearing without being crushed, without being full of anger, but instead being full of peace, knowing that we did what we could to see justice done, whether Ridge is released or not. And I will wait and watch to see just what good God might be working to accomplish on our behalf, and on Ridge's—if only Ridge will allow Him to do so—whether he is released or not.

My prayer will remain, through the hearing and until I get to hold Rebekah in my arms again:

Lord, please help us to be good witnesses for You. No matter what! Help us trust You and watch as You show Yourself faithful in a whole new realm of ways. Oh, how I love you, Father God, my Jesus, Holy Spirit. Thank You, thank You for loving me—even me!

AFTERWORD

Joseph

The phone call had not been meant for me, and yet I had been meant to answer it.

There is much more I could say about this. But I think the thing that sticks out the most is how tenderly those invisible hands dealt with me and my family. How we were spared many griefs, over and over again for years to come. I also watched those invisible hands not just protect but also comfort as they took on visible form in the love of friends and family. Even I, salty emanations having subsided, was also used in other ways.

What I hope that this book, my little part included, does is to convince you of the ever-present, though often unseen and unfelt, hands of loving-kindness. It was He who protected, empowered, and redeemed the situations and lives herein. He often shields, but not always. However,

He never abandons but always loves and stands ready to redeem—ready to refashion for good what is, in and of itself, so wrong and heartbreaking.

In closing, I am reminded of a letter that a dying man, who as a little boy had witnessed the death of his mother, wrote to a little girl: "If you continue to love Jesus, nothing much can go wrong with you, and I hope you may always do so."[12]

Joseph Gibson
Adjunct Faculty
Interdisciplinary Studies
Liberty University

---

[12] C. S. Lewis. Dorsett, Lyle W. and Marjorie Lamp Meade, eds., *C. S. Lewis: Letters to Children.* (New York: Touchstone, 2005), 111.

Safe in Your Arms

Saved by Grace

Waiting...

Illustrations by Lisa Peruchini

Nancy Jo Gibson graduated from James Madison University in Harrisonburg, Virginia, with a degree in early childhood education. She was once a Stonecroft speaker and has recently been the Soul Care and Biblical Guidance Director at her church. Since 2009, Nancy Jo has taken advantage of every opportunity to speak and minister to the abused, grieving, and incarcerated.

Today, she lives in the Shenandoah Valley with her husband, David, enjoying teas and other special outings with her six granddaughters. You can contact her by emailing AuthorNancyJo@gmail.com.